D0945079

If Horses Could Talk

'How a man saved his own life by talking to horses. And how he saved so many horses by understanding their language.'

If HORSES *could* TALK

Horse Whisperer

GARY WITHEFORD

with Brough Scott

RACING POST

First published in Great Britain in 2014
By Racing Post Books, 27 Kingfisher Court, Hambridge Road,
Newbury, Berkshire RG14 5SJ

10 9 8 7 6 5 4 3 2 1

A catalogue record for this book is available from the British Library.

ISBN 978-1-909471-69-6

Cover designed by Jay Vincent, text designed by J Schwartz & Co.

Printed and bound in the UK by CPI Group (UK) Ltd, Croydon, CR0 4YY

www.racingpost.com/shop

Photo Credits:
Stefan Forsman website: 110; Highclere Enterprises LLP: 151; John Hoy: plates two-2; Jo Hughes: 155; Darren Jack: front cover; Gavin James: plates one-6/7/8, 214, 215, 216, 219,221, 223, 224, 226, 228, 229, 230, 231, 233, 234, 235, 236(bottom), 239, 240; Sally Oliphant: 148; Joanna Petrie: 155; Racing Post/Edward Whitaker: plates one-6/7/8, 18, 29, 114, 183, 192, 194, 199, 200, 210, 225, 236(top), 237

Contents

Prologue

He was the saddest horse I had ever seen. He was called Brujo, and he was a big grey Andalusian colt tied to a concrete wall, with barbed wire round his nose and a boy stood alongside with his arm in a sling. They said the colt was crazy. That he had tried to kill the boy. That all he did was buck, buck, buck. That he was going to be shot for meat that evening.

I just saw this beautiful horse standing lost and rejected, with this awful barbed-wire thing round his nose. He was a big grey and I thought, what a wonderful creature. It was a magical moment. It was a hot day near Girona in north-east Spain, and I was down there with my friends Brian and Susie Oakley, who were looking for Andalusian fillies for their stud in Hertfordshire. The one they liked was in the field, but nobody could catch it and it had not yet been broken. So I just said to the bloke there, 'Look: if I can catch that filly and break it and get your son – your other son – on it and ride it away within 20 minutes, I'll have the colt you're going to shoot.' The man was so sure it wouldn't happen that he agreed.

All I had in my hand was the special rope halter I always use, and the Spaniards just laughed at me. But I went out to the filly, caught her, brought her back to their ménage, and began working her round the ring in the way I do. In the old way of doing things this 'breaking-in' process takes three to four weeks, but within 20 minutes I had the boy on her and she was being ridden away. To be fair, the man was very impressed and came and shook my hand.

I went over to Brujo, unchained him and took the barbed-wire thing off his nose. I put my rope halter on him and you could feel the air come out of him. It was just relief. They still said. 'You'll never do anything with him, because he's mad and dangerous.' I did not believe them. I think every horse deserves another chance, and I could see he had been abused. But I knew I could help him. Because I had been abused too.

For horses everywhere

'In my eyes horses could not hurt me, humans could.'

01 | Threatened Childhood

Gary Witheford is now a big, burly, blond stallion of a man. Put him together with even the most fractious horse, and within minutes he will have found a dialogue as simple and inspiring as you will ever see. Today he is the ultimate master of coaxing high-mettled thoroughbreds into the shaking steel cages of the starting-stalls, but he also continues to solve apparently hopeless cases of ordinary riding horses gone crooked. While this summer Gary has led a Classic winner and four Royal Ascot winners into the stalls and been interviewed on TV before the Derby, he has also, right in front of my eyes, redeemed the bronco-bucking problems of a handsome thug called Winston who was absolutely in the last-chance saloon.

But for all the success, the demonstrations, the website, the TV programmes and newspaper features, occasionally you can catch a look in Gary Witheford's very blue eyes that speaks of troubles in the past. Many of the horse problems will have been created by the ignorance of their owners: Gary's came from evil in one of its most insidious, unalloyed forms. Child abuse. This book is his testament to the havoc that abuse at such an early age has sometimes caused in his dealings with the human species, and the haven he then found in his life-giving work with horses. Indeed, it is out of his youthful traumas that Gary has found an empathy with horses, the truth of which is a much-needed lesson for all of us who profess to love them.

Not that there were any horses around during a childhood that became increasingly difficult. Gary was born at RAF Cosford in Shropshire on 28 April 1960, the second of what would be Jean and Bill Witheford's four sons. Corporal Witheford was a long-serving communications technician with the RAF, a short, active, man's man with a love of cars, bikes and deep-sea fishing. Home life was itinerant, with the family moving from one RAF base to another; Gary's parents' marriage, seemingly loveless, hardly helped, and he was always something of a hyperactive, attention-seeking child. 'Bring us boys round,' recalls Gary's younger brother Chris wryly, 'and within five minutes there would be a crash out the back and Gary would be in trouble.'

But these problems were nothing compared to what happened when the family moved to Singapore. At the Changi base where the family lived were twin brothers Reg and Tom Blakeley, fellow servicemen and, as Scout leaders and church officials, pillars of the community. In the classic 'grooming' way, the twins infiltrated themselves into the household, and began to abuse Gary. Unknown to him, his brothers would be abused too: four lives each scarred for eternity. The Blakeleys' ties with the family became even closer when they all returned to the UK. What was happening may have 'not seemed right' to the scared little boy, but it also didn't seem possible to complain about grown-ups who had become almost part of the family.

Gary wanted somewhere to escape to: something to love. More than anything, something to love him back. In some ways he has been searching ever since. He didn't know anything about horses, but he liked the idea of them. He was prepared to trust them. But with the first one, a pony, he ended up quite literally in the shit.

Brough Scott

It was a white pony, not very big – about 12 hands. It belonged to Ken the milkman. I used to help him on the milk round. I was about 11 then, back from Singapore, and we were living at RAF Rudloe Manor in Wiltshire, in one of those semi-detached services 'married quarters'. Ken and Ann, who also worked for the dairies, lived nearby in a cottage in Box, and had horses. Ken loved to go to Bath races. Ann knew I liked horses, although I had never ridden properly or anything, and so one evening she stuck me on this pony and took me riding with them.

Looking back it was a pretty stupid thing for them to do, but here I was on this pony, with Ann turning round and saying, 'You just walk and we are going to hack on.' Off they went, jumping the ditches on the grass verge beside the road before turning into the field. After they had gone about 400 yards this pony took off, with me who didn't even know how to do the rising trot. I promise you we must have jumped about ten of these ditches at full pelt, and then went into the field. I did not know where I was going: I was just clinging on to the saddle – I was almost screaming. We went right round the field, headed for the farm yard and then galloped straight into the slurry pit, and I was buried head-first in liquid cow shit. There was no one around when I got back to our house, so I took all my clothes off outside and went in and had a bath – no showers then. You would have thought it would have put me off horses for good. But I felt strangely elated.

Afterwards, I started doing things like getting on the two ponies down in a field near Rudloe Manor. There was a grey one and a bay one. I never saw them ridden, so I just got up on them and rode them round this little paddock. I did it quite often, and it was there that I first learned to ride a bit, kicking them around the field and shooing them along with a piece of rope. I could almost do the rising trot. Then the officer who owned them retired and moved them down to a field in Box, and I used to go down there on my bike and play Cowboys and Indians with his daughters. We would take it in turns riding the two horses between the three of us.

Somehow – I don't know why – I always felt I wanted to be close to horses, even though as a family we had no connection with them. I suppose I might have sat on a donkey at a beach, but I think it was my uncle Billy Johnston who put horses my way. He lived at Fordhouses in Wolverhampton, and he used to go to the pub of a Saturday saying, 'I am going to feed the horses', and do a Yankee on the races. One day he took me down the canal and there were horses there. I will never forget it: the first time I ever properly touched a horse.

You see, as an RAF family we weren't really allowed pets. I did once have a pet hamster, but it died after six weeks. In Upavon we had a pet rabbit because the kid who had it died of leukaemia – but then the rabbit died as well. My mother was not an animal lover, but my father told me that when he was a boy he had an Old English Sheep Dog. There weren't any animals to play with in Singapore but I used to sit and watch Westerns just to see the horses. I was fascinated at how the cowboys used to gallop around on them and just leap off and leave them standing still. There were horses when we got back to Wiltshire, and at Rudloe Manor there were lovely fields all around the base and we boys would stand on the gate and call the horses. They would not come to the others, but for some reason they would always come to me. Of course, I didn't really understand, but I was being hurt: I was being abused. In my eyes horses could not hurt me, humans could.

They say most people can remember when they were four years old, but I can actually remember long before that, of being in the pram screaming my head off, wanting to get out of

My first memory is of being in a pram and left. I hated it. I have been claustrophobic ever since.

the pram, and being left. In those days, you let the baby cry itself to sleep. I can remember not crying to sleep. I can remember going to a psychiatrist as a kid because I was strange – really I was just crying for help. I can remember that distinctly. I hated being on my own and being put into a pram and left. I can't remember my mother ever, *ever* giving me a kiss as a child, or putting her arm around me, or picking me up or anything. Maybe she did not mean it, and it must have been very hard bringing up four boys only five years apart, but I became the disruptive one and she could not handle me. Sometimes when I was difficult she would lock me in the coal bunker and leave me there until my father got home.

One day in Singapore – I'll never forget this because I'd obviously been a little shit or done something – it was a Sunday morning, and I'd obviously been playing my mother up, because she went to hit me: she was a right one to hit me with

Four Witheford boys in Singapore – *l–r* Chris, Kevin, me and Rob.

wooden spoons and belts and things like that. I put my hand up to stop being hit, but I had been playing darts and had three darts in my hand. They went right into her, and she had to go to hospital.

She told my dad that I'd stabbed her, which I hadn't. My father got hold of me. I was in bed at the time, and I can remember to this day him getting hold of me and pushing and holding my head in the pillow. I actually thought I was going to die. I couldn't breathe. He just pinned me down. It's the first time I felt the power of a man, of another person – of being scared.

My father was not very big but he was very strong. I remember him lifting an engine out of a Hillman Imp all by himself. He was a bit of an action man, and he'd go go-kart racing, he was a high diver – we've photos of him bloody rock-diving. He was really a Teddy boy from Birmingham, and he was hard. One day in the Angling Club at Changi I saw him fight and nearly kill a man. The guy had been giving my mother some gyp or something, and I remember my dad sitting on his shoulders and hitting him in the head. He knocked his teeth out and smashed his cheekbone in and it took four or five blokes to pull my dad off him. Yes he was strong.

My dad, RAF Corporal Bill Witheford – 'a bit of an action man'.

Of course I must have been disruptive. At Upavon I remember burning down a

Visiting family in Wales – four boys and no motorways! I am the one with the dog.

hedge behind the NAAFI, which was not very clever, and I got a hell of a hiding. Yet some of it was me being misunderstood. My brothers will tell you of the day I cut all the car leads, but I was just trying to be a mechanic like my dad. In many ways I think he would have been much happier if one of his children had been a daughter. It would have softened him a bit although he remained a hero to us all and a lot of things were good, especially in Singapore, where we used to go swimming and sea fishing. But it was there we met Reg and Tom.

They were also in the RAF, and they brought their mother out from Bournemouth and became friends of the family. They were absolutely identical twins, quite tall and good-looking, and from the outside were real do-gooders. They were always very involved in the church, and one ran the Scouts and the other did the Cubs. Of course, we did not realise it, but looking back they were working their way in all the time.

As typical of what they do, I can remember being in a camp in Malaysia with the Cubs. It was like a Jamboree sort of thing, and I must have been eight years old. Do you know when you get up a bit quick and you get that dizzy feeling? I can remember bending down to get some soap or my flannel off the floor. I got up really quick and I sort of, whoa – Reg was behind me. That's the very first time I felt – sensed – that there was something wrong, because he came over and stroked my neck. He started to rub my neck. He said, 'Oh, you'll be OK', and things like that. That was the first time that I actually felt, this isn't right. Being a kid, it just seemed wrong. I knew it was wrong.

Of the two, Tom was worse. Reg was more gentle, if you see what I mean. Tom was more of an aggressive player. He'd almost pin you down. When we got back to Rudloe Manor Tom was staying at our house. I think he had broken both his legs parachuting. He was in my brother's bedroom, and he was lying in bed with both legs like this in plaster. He just pinned me, and he started playing with me. That was the initial shock – when he got hold of my cock, sort of thing. He was all, like, it was good – and I was thinking, what's going on?

I can remember walking out the house after that first time in the bedroom. It must have been the time of horse riding, things like that, of Ken and Ann. It must have been that sort of time, because that's when I started throwing myself into horses properly as in getting out because I didn't want to go home.

But I was powerless, and Tom began to do it more and more. Unknown to me he was doing it to most of the others as well, and so was Reg. Tom would do it to me under the table. I remember one Christmas Day we were having lunch and he was playing with my penis under the table. I could not believe no one noticed. It felt as if they didn't care.

At the time it was happening to me as a kid everything got quite strange, to the point where you knew inside this was wrong but these were adults, and friends of the family. It couldn't be wrong. These were people you looked up to. It's a funny feeling to this day. I had three to four years counselling, although not until after my father had died. I would have been 34, 35 when it all came to light properly, so you can imagine how repressed it must all have been.

I did stupid things like running away and people had to come and find me. When more houses were being built at Rudloe Manor, I hid in the drain. My father gave me a slap when they found me. It was, 'Typical Gary' – just defiant. I was always quarrelling with my brother Kevin. I was always seen as the difficult one. Finally my parents felt I was too disruptive at weekends – so they sent me down to stay with Tom and Reg's mother in their house in Poole, and there Reg started on me as well.

Reg did it a different way from Tom. He was a soft man, he did it slowly: he would give you a cuddle. Down in his mother's house in Poole, he got into bed with me. Tom had got into bed first. I was playing as if I was dead. To this day I can remember: Tom was fiddling around with me under the bedclothes, and then an alarm went off because Tom had to go off to work. And as soon as he had left, Reg came in.

One day they both took me out in a boat, and when they started on me I was so frightened that I jumped overboard and swam ashore. Nobody would understand why I hated going down there. I remember pulling the curtain in our bedroom off the tracks as my father tried to drag me away. It was just Gary being difficult again.

All my brothers went to a school in Corsham, the normal comprehensive school. I went to Cardinal Newman's in Bath – I had to leave earlier than the others, come back later – because I needed to be separated from my older brother Kevin, because I was disruptive to the family, which is quite heart-breaking looking back to what the real reasons were. Finally I was sent off to this special state boarding school in Devizes. I think I just felt that things could only get better. Thanks to Alan Stonell they did.

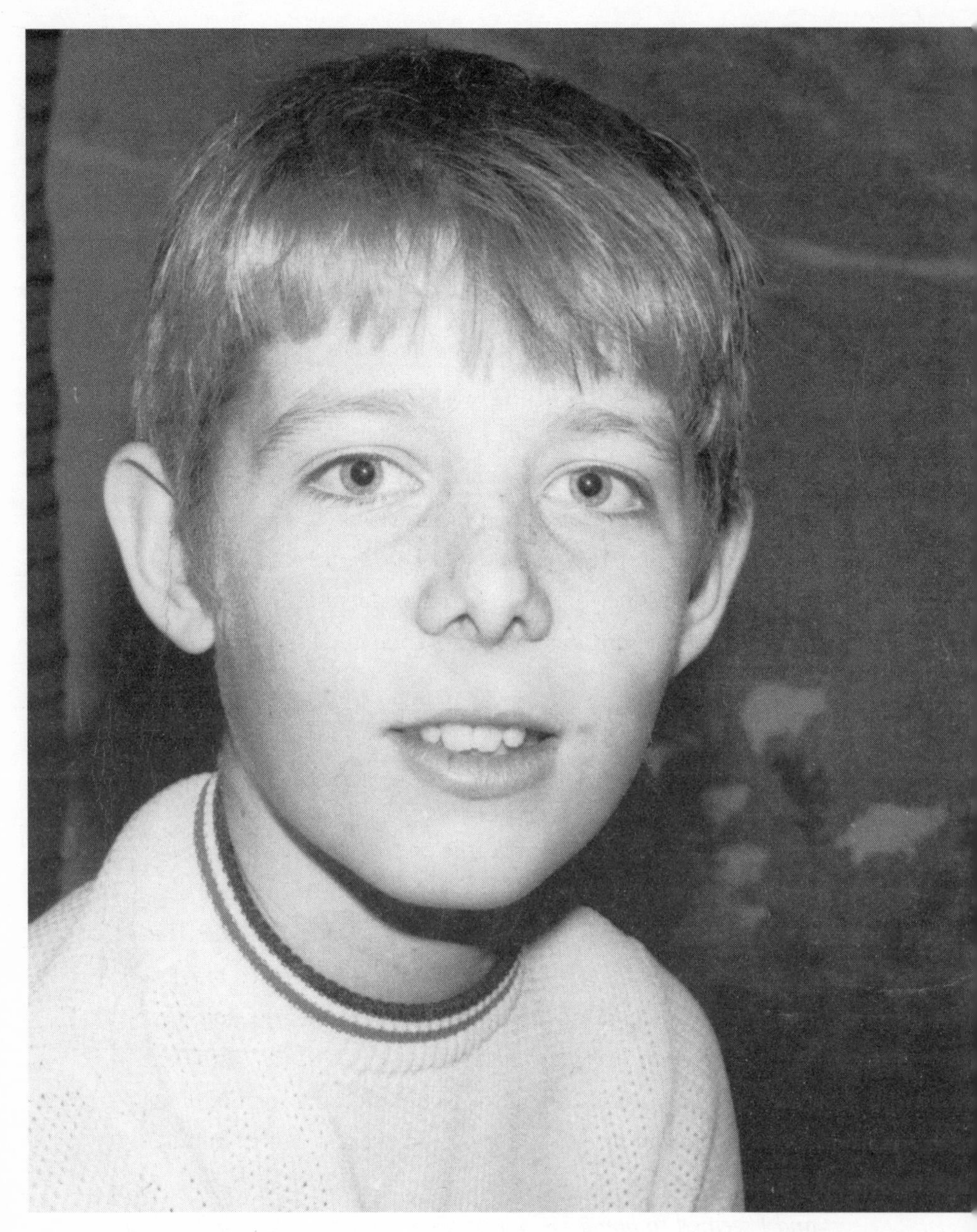

'At home I was always being treated as trouble, here I was part of something.'

02 | School of Salvation

Alan Stonell was a happily married man with a son a couple of years younger than Gary, adept at making things, handling animals – he had been in the RAF's Police Dog Demonstration Team – and beekeeping. A prize-winning carpentry apprentice, he had become a woodwork teacher, and when Trowbridge Technical College closed in 1971 he got a job at Downland, a state boarding school in Devizes newly opened for boys who needed special attention. He was the sort of master every child and every parent prays for.

Alan still lives in Devizes, in a well-ordered semi on a modest estate. In 2004, after years of nursing her, he lost his wife to cancer, and though his subsequent desire to become a minister in the church was thwarted by his age, the unsung good works continue. He still runs educational courses at the Wiltshire Beekeeping Association – there are busy hives in the back garden and 'guest' ones out the front ready to home any errant swarm in need of relocation. The local school kids are bound for the Salisbury Choirs Festival and it is Alan Stonell who has been part of getting them there.

'I think Gary was having some trouble at home, and Mum and Dad were having problems,' Alan recalls gently. But to him Gary could confide that the trouble at home was something more. 'He and I seemed to bond. He got on well with my son, and he liked to help me with the bees and other things. And he had this thing

about horses – in the dormitory he had pictures of one above his bed. One of the masters, Bill Warmington, always walked around with the Sporting Life *in his pocket, and he knew the people at the stables at Beckhampton. Another boy small enough to be a jockey used to go there at weekends, so they took Gary too. It worked for him.'*

Beckhampton, just six miles from Devizes, is one of the great racing stables of the land, with a record of 41 English Classics including nine Derbys dating back to 1839. Such places are schools in their own right, with more pupils on four legs than on two, and to be part of them is to join a community infected with a uniquely inspiring madness: the belief that one of those four-legged pupils will one day be a name to conjure with. Even if Gary mostly just swept the yard, Alan had found him a touchstone. The never-ending process of recovery was under way.

'I don't want for anything,' said Alan as he saw me back to the car, 'but I do like helping other people. It is very good to see them make their way'. Years earlier he had given Gary the chance to find his own epiphany. On a horse.

She was called Cottontail. When she was a foal something had eaten her tail, and it was now not much more than a wisp of a thing – hence her name. She was a two-year-old, and she obviously wasn't much good, as she only ran twice, and so poorly that she was promptly sold to Australia. But to me she was something special. She was the first racehorse I ever sat on.

All I actually did was ride her back from the gallops at Beckhampton. That's what would happen to us kids: as a special treat, you would be taken up to gallops and allowed to ride a quiet one back after it had finished work. Cottontail might not have been any use on the track, but sitting on her was the first time I felt the size and power of the thoroughbred.

Alan Stonell got me to Beckhampton as he knew I liked horses, and we had another kid from school, Chris Fox, going there already because he was so small everyone thought he ought to be a jockey. The other boys had pictures of Leeds United players; I had ones of horses. Alan got the deputy head to arrange Beckhampton at the weekends because I couldn't go home. They were very good to me there. They got me a pair of secondhand jodphurs and I swept the yard, did mucking-out and odd jobs, and they put me on 'the Pony'. I slept in the dormitory with their apprentices, ate in the hostel and

Beckhampton. My first haven. In those days the trainer was Jeremy Tree. I still go there often for his successor Roger Charlton.

on Sundays we were given 50p to go and have lunch at the Waggon and Horses.

'The Pony' – I can't remember its name – was a cussed old thing and always running sideways and bucking me off. But it did not seem to discourage me. It seemed I had a purpose, and although I was very, very junior, when I was sitting in the canteen I was talking with grown-ups, and on Sundays I was actually in the pub with them. At home I felt I was always being treated as trouble: here I was part of something. Best of all I was sort of part of Cottontail. However silly it sounds, she became 'my horse'. When she ran at Salisbury there was her name in the papers, and I could say, 'I rode that.'

Beckhampton was a really gorgeous place. Very smart and old-fashioned – I can remember the smell even now. The smell of hay and horses and leather in the tack room. Jeremy Tree, the trainer, was very much a polite, old-school gentleman with a jacket and tie and often a waistcoat. He was quite fat: I always used to think he looked like an older Billy Bunter, and he used to have his binoculars slung over his shoulder. When he came round evening stables he would wear white gloves, and if he thought the horse was not perfect he would run his gloved finger down its back and say, 'Boy, has this horse been done over?'

Until I went to Downland, school life was becoming more and more difficult for me. Although the first reports I have from Upavon Primary don't look too bad, I remember being in Singapore when we had to do joined-up writing for the first time. I had never done it and could not copy it down fast enough before the master rubbed the line out. I had obviously got a bit of dyslexia, but all my family said was, 'You're thick, you're thick.' What made it more frustrating is that I had my brother Kevin at the top of the pecking order, and my mother and father saying what a fantastic lad he was, and there was me crying for help. I still get panic attacks thinking about it.

Downland was very different. There were only 40 of us in the school, all problem children, people who'd been abused or assaulted or beaten up, but there were always plenty of things to do. I never really liked football, although I was quite good at it and once scored a hat-trick. I preferred to do the beekeeping with Alan, to look after the chickens. I used to do anything with animals, and all the green, farming-type stuff. I loved carpentry and the metal work, and things like that. But we went off on all kinds of trips, too. We went trekking in Wales, sea fishing down in Cornwall, hiking in the Lake District, boating on the canals. I got a special commendation for being helpful. So I can't have been that bad a pupil, although to start with I was

Me at Downland. There were always plenty of things to do.

very distrustful, even of Alan – for a while I actually wondered if he might be after me too.

So it took some time for him to win my confidence. He just seemed to befriend me. We talked and talked. He invited me round to see his wife and kids in his flat at the end of our block.

My saviour at Downland, Alan Stonell, his wife and daughter.

Slowly he got it out of me what was happening at home, and I broke. But I only broke about Tom. I didn't break about Reg because he was a more gentle person. I think I felt more intimidated by Tom, as a kid more scared of him.

Anyway, the shit hit the fan. I can remember this Friday walking into the headmaster's office and being made to sit at the end of the desk alongside Alan and opposite the headmaster. My father comes in, and who is with him but Reg. There is me accusing Reg's brother of interfering with me, knowing that Reg has interfered with me too. So it was quite scary. I was only 13, and thinking 'What the **** do I do here?' I remember

Reg saying, 'Go on', and Alan saying, 'Go on, keep talking.' But I couldn't. I'm filling up now even thinking about it.

I can remember being asked to leave the room. I went out and had to stand in the secretary's office – literally stood outside. Then I was asked to come back in again. Mr Lawrence, who was the headmaster, said, 'We are going to handle this. Your father wants it dealt with quietly. He's going to go back and Reg is going to have a word with his brother to make sure it never happens again.' That was it.

But it did happen again. Tom did keep away, but Reg was always around and would be doing it, although he was very different. Tom was a pervert – a forceful paedophile. He was dirty with it: frightening, scary. He would be the one to tell you he is going to kill your dog, so don't tell your parents. But Reg was a very gentle man: he would do it discreetly and then apologise the next day. I can remember coming back from Poole and him telling me, 'Don't say anything about this – it should not have happened.' Even from the beginning in Singapore, when nothing actually happened, I knew something wasn't right. People say to me, why didn't you go and beat them up, because they have taken your innocence? But as a child you were in awe of them. Even to this day, if they walked in through the gate, I would still feel intimidated by them. Yet if someone did that to my kids, I would kill them.

These days, if you mention somebody has touched your leg or something the social services would be brought in. But back then such things were treated very differently. They were hushed up. I felt betrayed and dirty. I felt absolutely as if even my father could not stand up for me. It meant I wanted to go home even less.

Alan realized this, although I still did not tell him about Reg. He could also see how much I enjoyed going to Beckhampton, and as I was getting a lot bigger than Chris Fox, Alan was being told that I really needed to go to a jumping stable. Mr Warmington had some contact with Stan Mellor, and so I was taken over there by Alan to meet him and his wife Elain. They said I could come for the weekends and holidays. That would change my life just as much.

'I had my dog and I was happy. Sheba was my friend and so were my horses.'

03 | Safety in a Stable

By 1974 standards Linkslade Racing Stable on the Wantage Road half a mile out of Lambourn in Berkshire was an enlightened place. In Stan and Elain Mellor they had a fresh and charismatic couple at the head of affairs, she bright and sociable, he a hugely respected former champion jockey. They had influential owners, an increasing number of horses, a decent stable lads' hostel. And, from the summer of that year, they also had Gary Witheford.

Stan Mellor was already making a name for himself as a trainer three years after ending a career which in December 1971 had seen him become the first jockey to ride a thousand winners over jumps. His ability in the saddle and his much-applauded work for his fellow riders meant he already had a bank of good will, good owners and horses to match. As a foil to his talents he had, in Eric Wheeler, a tough, uncompromising head lad deeply steeped in the fundamentals of the game.

Stan and Elain now live half a dozen miles from Lambourn in a pleasant cottage filled with memorabilia in the village of Ashbury, nestling in the shoulder of the Swindon side of the Berkshire Downs. Stan is an even sparer figure now than he was during his riding and training career, and a hearing-aid and a new knee and set of teeth are witnesses to the ravages of battle. But he and Elain are quick to pull down the scrapbooks and check the progress of the quiet, fair-haired little boy who started so shyly under their wing.

'The schoolmaster [Alan Stonell] was very good,' remembers Elain. 'He never told us about Gary's problems – just that he could not go home very easily. At first he just brought him over for the weekends, and then he came for the whole summer holidays. Looking back I do remember how attentive he was with his horses. Some boys just do what they are told – often not even that. But Gary was different. He was quiet, but I think he was quiet because he was so totally absorbed in the animals. He didn't need any more of that hyperactivity. He was like a sponge, learning from people like Eric and the experienced lads. It was obvious he was fascinated. He could not do enough for his horses.'

Full-time work could not start until Gary left school at 16, but in the meantime he would get £2 a week pocket money and, in preparation, do the six-week apprentices' course up at Stoneleigh in Warwickshire under the Mellors' sponsorship. For a boy whose actual home life appeared increasingly dysfunctional, a ladder was being held up to something better.

The Mellor connection was to last 11 years. Many things, both professional and personal, would grow from it. But nothing would ever erase the memory of Gary's 'first fine careless rapture': the first time he sat on a racehorse at the gallop.

I will never forget the feeling. Daily Aide was a big chestnut: a beautiful, beautiful chestnut. He was the first horse I had a real bond with, and here he was galloping beneath me up the wood shavings at Lambourn. It was the first time I had ridden a racehorse in a 'canter'. I couldn't believe the feeling and the power of this horse.

Eric Wheeler had taken me across to the bottom of the canter that runs for nearly a mile alongside the Wantage Road and said, 'Right, you are coming with me, and if you get run away with there is a gate into a ploughed field at the top of the hill. That will stop him.' He had given me one of his caps – remember, we didn't use helmets in those days – and I turned it round and off we set. When we got to the top, I turned it back again.

Daily Aide was wonderful. He was an absolute Christian. He used to carry his neck and head so low that his chin was hitting the grass. Here is the first thoroughbred I have 'cantered' on, and his head has disappeared! You think, 'Jesus, where's it gone?' It was peculiar, but I just left him alone and he lobbed up behind Eric. But the biggest thing was that he taught me how to canter. I used to say to him, 'Whoa, now,' and he would stop at the end of the gallop. He just knew his job. It was fantastic. I can remember riding back along the road afterwards. Don't forget, most kids, especially in racing, would have been galloping all their life. But I hadn't. I felt great. I couldn't get enough of it. I wanted to go again.

Daily Aide did win a race, but he was not much of a racehorse, and I never looked after him properly – just had him whenever I came out of school. He was given to me because he was the quietest horse in the yard, but I thought he was wonderful. I would play with him in the box; he would never put a foot wrong. It did something for me. There was this horse, this big chestnut horse, touching me without hurting me in any way, and I would stroke him back, just him and me. In the afternoons I would go up to the gallops with a mucksack and pick him clover. He was lovely. That was when I first began to find that the more time you put into horses, the more you get back. I think I learned then that they've actually got brains. They're all individuals and they are all different, like you and me.

To be honest, I was finding most of this out by myself. The next summer holidays I was sent up to the Apprentice School at Stoneleigh, and it nearly put me off. I was the youngest boy on the course – I was only 14 – and that meant I was bullied a bit. There were some good moments: it was the time of the Royal Show and they had a swimming pool as part of it, so at night we would crawl under the canvas into the marquee, strip off and swim there. One night the other boys nicked my and another lad's clothes, so we had to run back through Stoneleigh stark bollock-naked.

It was the actual riding that was not much fun. You would be made to go round this school on an old racehorse that would cut across the corner and throw you off, and then you would get shouted at. It was the same day after day. Johnny Gilbert, the guy who ran the place, had been a top hurdles jockey, and he would slap and bang us when he was showing us how to ride a finish:

Stan and Elain Mellor. I was with them for eleven years.

'Put your arms here, get your arse down, make your back flat.' By the time I returned to Stan's I had almost had enough of it.

But I was young and I loved working in the yard and riding out. I would start early because I couldn't wait. At night I used to sneak out of the hostel, run round to the tack room, and I'd manage to open one of the windows so I could see what I was to ride in the morning. I hated it if I was just on a walker and not going up to the gallops.

Stan and Elain, and Eric in his own way, seemed pleased with me, so when school finished I joined them full-time. I was already getting too heavy, so I signed up not as an apprentice or a conditional jockey but as a stable lad. I got the regular wage at the time. It was £10 a week. Well, it was better than two shillings' pocket money.

I was the newest kid on the block, so I don't suppose anybody thought they were doing me any favours in two of the horses they gave me to look after. There was a ten-year-old called Alpenstock who had never won a race, and a big black thing called Baltic Love that was lame half the time. They were mine to look after, but nobody thought they would be any good.

Alpenstock wasn't very big but he was strong, by that famous old stallion Vulgan, and he was one of those lovely light bays with a black mane and tail. He had a nice broad head but, Jesus, he used to buck. He had a hell of a buck for a ten-year-old. He was a fantastic horse, second to none. He was a good ride, but you had to watch out when he was fresh, like on a Monday morning or a work morning, when the horses knew they were going to work because they were going up that Seven Barrows Road. You would have to hold on to him because he'd dump you – just before you went on to the gallop he used to whip round to the left and stick one in. He was pretty good at that. A few times he dumped me – he dumped some of the best: even Steve Jobar, the stable jockey, came off him. He was a bugger for bucking: he could stick a buck in – and whip round. My, he could whip round! – he dropped me once and put me through a barbed-wire fence, and I promise you I had just bought a brand new pair of jodhpurs, and those jodhpurs were something like three weeks' wages.

But Alpenstock was great to deal with in the box and everywhere. He was an absolute Christian. I loved him to bits – it was almost pathetic to know how much I loved that horse. I learnt so much from him: I learnt that they have got souls; they have got their own thoughts. And I am convinced horses know when they win, too: some people say they don't, but look at Alpenstock. He came to us as a ten-year-old maiden and had been racing since he was two years old. Then he started getting it together. He won at Doncaster and Worcester: he had so much confidence in himself. In March 1977 I took him to Cheltenham and he won the amateur's National Hunt Handicap Chase ridden by Dick Saunders, who later won the 1982 Grand National on Grittar. There I was, still just 16 years old and leading in a winner at the National Hunt Festival! The one thing that pissed me off was that when we got to the actual unsaddling enclosure the owner pushed in and led Alpenstock in himself. I felt it was not his horse but mine.

For a kid it was an extraordinary day, but from a family point of view what had happened at Wolverhampton a month earlier was almost better. For the other horse I did beside Alpenstock was that big black thing, Baltic Love. He was a cripple. He would be lame half the time but he seemed to be getting better. When I was leading him round the paddock at Wolverhampton, there leaning against the rails was Uncle Billy and his brother John, and John's wife Maureen, who was the first woman ever to give me a cuddle. She and the others had always believed in me. 'Will he win?' said Uncle Billy. I said, 'Yeah, get on,' and they all went off and backed him. Baltic Love never won another race but that day in he came at 10-1. They thought it was Christmas.

Baltic Love was important to me for another reason. He taught me the importance of 'strapping' horses at night – of feeling them all over. As I said, when I first had Baltic Love he seemed an absolute cripple, but there was an old boy in the yard called Frankie who showed me how to 'strap' him: he would have two really clean stable cloths and he would massage away, whistling through his teeth. That's what 'strapping' is. Everyone used to do it years ago, but now only Frankie really did. It meant you worked your hands all over his body, all over the muscles in his shoulder, and along his flanks. You would push your fingers into his skin and feel the fibres respond. I found Baltic Love really liked it. He would lean in to me as I did it. If he had been a cat he would have purred. He was never a good mover but he did get better, and I am sure the strapping made a difference.

I did it with every horse I had: they liked it; they relaxed. With Baltic Love I learned that horses would be scared when you first went *bang, bang,* with the rubber. They jump away, especially a young horse. They jump and then find what you are doing is actually quite nice. They start to lean into you and start to relax with you. So it's the same principle when I'm working horses who are scared of everything, who jump away at boards and people and clippers and things like that. I learned if you keep going to them and stop them running away from the problem they will realise they don't need to be frightened of it. It's what we call 'de-flighting': it 'desensitises' them: stops them jumping away when you touch them or even approach. What doesn't work is if you stop the moment the horse jumps away: that teaches them that jumping away from you makes you stop.

Take clipping, for instance. In a jumping yard every horse bar the odd thin-skinned young colt needs clipping in the autumn when his winter coat comes through, and unless you do it, he sweats buckets at exercise. So you've got your clippers, you walk into the stable, and as soon as you turn your clippers on the horse will jump away. So you go, 'S*** – I'll get some ACP to tranquilise him.' Actually, it's the wrong thing to do. You've just taught that horse to be scared of clippers, because when he jumped you took the clippers away. What you should do is go on up to him, *buzz, buzz, buzz,* touch him once, and only when he stands still instead of climbing up the wall do you turn it off. He learns that when he stands still the pressure comes off. When you turn it on again, he won't climb up the wall. I wasn't to know it, but it was part of Pressure and Release, which is at the heart of how I communicate with horses. As I see it, a horse is an animal of flight. That is why it will jump away from you when it is scared. But if you cut off that flight it will become passive: it will accept you as its leader. That's when you can start to do things with it – in this case, clipping. That was all beginning to form in my head as I strapped Baltic Love every night.

Frankie was a great old guy. He and his mate Mac were called 'the Old Codgers', and only used to come in and work the mornings. One day in November 1984 Frankie dropped dead in the yard with a muck sack on his back. We know it was November because the Lord Lucan story hit the papers next day. Frankie was never famous, but he was special to me and to the horses I did.

But I now had another animal. The first thing I did when I came to the Mellors full-time was to go up to Stan and ask if I could borrow £90 in advance of my wages. Because it was to buy an Old English Sheep Dog puppy he lent me the money. I got her from a puppy farm near Henley and called her Sheba. She used to come everywhere with me: in the hostel, in the horse box – later she even came to my wedding. My father, you remember, used to tell me that as a child he had had an Old English Sheep Dog that used to pull a cart with the milk in it: looking back, I think my buying that puppy was another cry for help – wanting my parent to love me.

Ninety quid was a hell of a lot of money then – about two months' wages. I paid it off by working extras. I would go racing whenever I could and get £2 a day for leading one up [preparing a horse for its race and leading it round the paddock] or a fiver if it was an overnight. I used to polish shoes – 25p or 50p for a pair of shoes: the lads would sleep in the afternoon and

My dog Sheba. She was my best friend.

leave their boots outside like in a hotel. On Sunday afternoons some of them would not want to come back from the pub and would ring the call box in the hostel and say, 'Oh, Gary, could you do my horses tonight?' It would be, 'Thank you very much,' and £2 in my back pocket. They used to call me 'Shylock'.

Because of Sheba I never slept in the hostel and to begin with I lived in an old converted stable. It had a bed, a chair and a sink: the bed for me, the chair for Sheba, and the sink to wash in. When I wanted a bath I went to the corner room in the hostel where Steve Jobar lived, but I was scared to do that because there were rats running around in the roof. After that I had a caravan which was fine except when it rained, and I had to sit with buckets and bowls to catch the water leaking through the ceiling. On Christmas Eve my nan came up with my mother and Uncle Billy to give me my presents as I was working right through Boxing Day. When they left my nan was crying in the car, saying to my mother, 'How can you leave your boy in a place like that?' But Mum just said, 'He loves his horses.'

It was true. I had my dog and I was happy. Sheba was my friend but so were my horses. In all my time at Stan Mellor's every single horse I looked after won at least one race. Tell me that was just a coincidence.

'Every single horse I looked after won at least one race. Tell me that was just a coincidence.'

04 | Royal Mail

So what do we make of that good-looking, slightly reticent, mop-haired youth who looks out with his Old English Sheep Dog from the past? He was certainly an original: the purchase of Sheba after his very first pay packet told us that. He was fascinated by animals and by horses in particular. He was both energetic and an enduringly uncertain mix of calculation and impetuosity. Sometimes that quixotic nature makes you unsure whether to laugh or frown, or even cry.

You certainly have to laugh at the young Gary smoking undetected up a tree at Downland while the other boys kept getting caught doing the same thing behind the bike sheds. You can have an indulgent smile at the callow apprentice losing his virginity to an experienced and enthusiastic girl groom inside a giant display milk churn in the showground at Stoneleigh. But you might raise an eyebrow at how our engaging 15-year-old put his new-found carnal knowledge to use when he returned to Devizes. He began what appears to have been a full and mutually satisfying relationship with a still clearly very fit 39-year-old cleaning lady and mother of five whose husband worked in Scotland.

Full marks for originality, perhaps? At Downland he used to keep himself awake listening to Radio Luxembourg under the bed clothes, then sneak out through a window, hotfoot the half-mile to the lady's house, collect the key under the mat, and bingo. It all worked grand until the night there was no key because the husband had come home from Scotland. Amazingly, the trysts continued when Gary moved to Lambourn, and on various occasions our lady of the broom handle would make the not-inconsiderable taxi ride from Devizes. Maybe everyone thought she was his auntie?

But throughout his life, the only education in which Gary really graduated with honours was the one he had from horses. In addition to Alpenstock and Baltic Love, that attentiveness Elain Mellor had so immediately noticed was being applied to a tall grey ex-flat racer called Hipparion, and a nearly black chaser that, in light of its tearaway tendencies, was challengingly named Pacify.

He was a bastard to ride, Pacify. He was a black horse and very lean and awkward. He used to be so nervous in the box that he had a donkey called Jenny who even used to go to the races with him. He was horrible to canter, his neck straight up in the air, his head in your face. And on the gallops he would run away with everyone. No one could hold him except Jobi – Steve Jobar. Then there was this morning.

We were at the bottom of the gallops by the plantation opposite where Barry Hills is now. I had ridden Pacify up and we were waiting for Steve Jobar to arrive. Chris Glynn was already parked at the top of the gallop to watch Pacify work: he was a great owner and a very nice man who since he was 30 had been in a wheelchair after breaking his back diving into a hidden rock in Sydney Harbour. He had been driven over to watch his horse gallop, so gallop it would. But then Stan comes across and says, 'Right, Jobi's not turned up, so you'll have to ride Pacify.' Now that was a bombshell!

I'm a 16-year-old kid and I'm thinking, 'How am I going to hold this big, black, skinny thing with its head in the air and no brakes?' So as we rode down to the bottom of the gallop I thought, 'Right, you're going to run away with me, I'm going to ****ing go first. I'll chuck the reins at you and you can help yourself, and at least I should be able to pull up at the end.'

Well, you know what happened? He never even took a hold. We sailed up there. I quickened him up through the woods. He did the job absolutely perfect. After that I was always on his back. I rode him every day, in the school, out round the woods and everywhere.

That's what taught me a lot about what I now do. It's that Pressure and Release thing again. I was thinking, 'Hang on, if you want to pull me, how can I put the pressure on you? How can I' – who back then was probably under nine stone – 'hold a horse of half a ton with its head up in the air?' So I just dropped my hands on him: that was 'release', and he was fine. From that day I have never, ever, been run away with.

After that I got to ride a lot of the nutters at Stan's, but I did get some terrific horses to do, not just Pacify, who in the end won eight races including the Midlands Grand National. Hipparion was great, and took me all over the place, winning races on the flat as well as over hurdles. He won a good race at Goodwood one day ridden by Elain. I did a nervous sort of horse called In View, who taught me a lot about this thing I call 'de-flighting.' He used to worry and walk his box, and people used to tie him up tighter and tighter to try and stop him. But I let him have a loose rope and used to talk to him. It seemed to get him to relax and he became quite good in the end. He won a nice race for me at Haydock with Steve Jobar riding.

But the best horse I did – just about the best horse anyone ever did – was Royal Mail. He came up from New Zealand in the spring of 1978. Stan was always thinking ahead of the game, and the year before a whole shipment of horses had arrived to sell on – so many that for a while we did not have enough stables, and had to put two horses in the same box. There was a

With Royal Mail – I was so proud of him.

good horse among them called Explorateur, and when Philip Blacker won on him at Sandown we all won a lot of money and the owner came round and gave £50 to everyone in the yard – we thought he was a star, but he got busted as a drug dealer and went to jail.

But Royal Mail lasted. He was a big pale chestnut with a long white blaze down his face and white stockings right up to his hocks. He had come up from the Southern Hemisphere summer so he had his summer coat – he was stunning: I loved to stroke him. We had heard about him – he had been a really good horse in New Zealand, won six races and been one of their top hurdlers – but when he arrived with us he had been a disappointment. Here was the most terrible mover you ever saw. He was stiff and he was sour. I had been looking forward to him, but this almost seemed as if someone was playing a joke on me. Looking back, though, I am sure his problems were pain-related. I used to talk to him in the box, scrape bits of carrot and add them to his feed, and gradually became mates with him. In the end I got to where he would just walk out after me with a head collar on and I would take him up to the paddock to get a pick of grass. He became very friendly.

He had terrible joints and knees, so I used to ice them and cold-hose them on a regular basis, and take him down to stand in the river just before you get to the square in Lambourn. He would love his pick of grass in the afternoons, and on some days I would ride him down to the swimming pool at Windsor House on the other side of the village. He was so stiff to start with that I guess he probably had slightly kissing spines. These days you could have given him a cortisone injection and he would have been fine, but back then nobody thought about that. We just had to do everything we could.

It was from Royal Mail I learned about working a horse loose. The automatic horse-walkers we had then were of the 'tether' kind, where the horse is tied to the front of the moving barrier on what was really a turning carousel like you see in a fairground. But with that system, if the horse got clever it could drag back, and stop the machine moving. Royal Mail was clever: 'warming him up' on the horse-walker didn't work because he would stop the sodding thing. So, ten minutes before we would be due to pull out in the mornings, I would take him up to our covered school to loosen him up. I used to call him 'Malley', as in Royal Mail. 'Trot on, Malley,' I would say. I used to stand on the corner and he would trot round in front of me.

He would listen to your voice and watch your body language. When he was at the furthest point away he could have stopped, but he didn't. I shouted to him and he just kept on trotting round on his own. He had the saddle and bridle on and everything, but it was as if he knew what he had to do. And when the first lot came out, I used to call him up – 'Come on, Malley' – and he used to trot up to me. He was just like those Western horses I had seen on the TV in Singapore. I would jump on him and away we would go, and because of his back and his stiffness I would always stand up in the irons for the first 30 or 40 strides to ease the pressure on his spine. After a bit we got him a special saddle to fit over his very high wither. Steve Jobar made it: it was the first saddle he ever did.

Royal Mail was terribly talented. You could work him with flat horses. Second time out he was third to Sea Pigeon and Bird's Nest in the Fighting Fifth Hurdle at Newcastle, and two races later he was in front and might have won if he had not fallen at the third last in the King George VI Chase at Kempton on Boxing Day. When we had him he won the Whitbread, he broke the track record at Gowran Park in Ireland, he was third in the National, second in the Gold Cup – at one time I thought he could win everything. He would get Christmas cards. He had a fan club. He had a woman who used to follow him around at the races: she had fallen in love with the horse – she used to bring packets of Polos and stand by the paddock.

Philip Blacker had become stable jockey and he was talented, too. His father had been head of the army or something and had won races over fences and show-jumped for Britain on a horse called Workboy. But he was also a painter, and Philip inherited that artistic talent to become a brilliant sculptor: when he retired the first thing he did was a bronze of Royal Mail. Philip was tall, with curly fair hair, and he used to talk with a sort of breathless laugh when we were thinking of things we could do with our horses. We used to talk about Royal Mail a lot. This horse has too much speed to be a real three-mile chaser, I always used to say, and while he did finish second in the Gold Cup in 1979 he was out on his feet, and in truth he was getting tired when he fell in the race the next March. That's what made it all the more amazing that Royal Mail could win the Whitbread over three miles, five furlongs a month later – and that just six weeks after breaking his jaw at Cheltenham.

When I got to him that day in 1980 he was bleeding from both nostrils and from his mouth. I thought he'd knocked a tooth out, but he hadn't. Walking him back, you could see that the whole of his jaw was beginning to swell. When I was washing him down he was pretty stressed, because there was a lot of pain. The vet looked at him and said, 'He's broken his jaw: there's nothing we can do about it – it doesn't warrant wiring or pinning; it will just set itself and grow a callus.' They didn't have mobile X-rays in those days, so Royal Mail and I just went back to Lambourn in the horse box. The next morning the lower jaw was very swollen. The poor old bugger was in a lot of pain and could hardly eat. I went and picked grass for him as at least he could get some of that down.

He lost a bit of condition, but we used to mince up his food and I would shake it around in an old Coca-Cola bottle and pour it straight down his throat. Obviously we could not put a bit in his mouth, so I rode him out in just a head collar. The horse was really sensible, and when it came to the Whitbread we made Philip a bit-less bridle and put blinkers on to help focus him. People say winning over that distance proved he stayed, but Philip says that because there was no great gallop

Leading Royal Mail and Philip Blacker in at Sandown after winning the 1980 Whitbread Gold Cup in a bit-less bridle six weeks after breaking his jaw at Cheltenham.

it worked to Royal Mail's advantage: at the end he was just too fast for the rest of them. We were very proud of him that day. It was a big, big race. He was on the TV and in all the papers. I was part of him. For the first time in my life I was sort of important.

Going up to Aintree with him the next year was the ultimate, and quite a worry, too. For the Grand National was a scary thing: we had lost horses in it. One year we had a horse called Beau Bob killed in it, and there was a picture of him landing on his head at Becher's Brook just before he died. Because Royal Mail was always so stiff he needed a lot of strapping, and before that first National in 1981 I can remember strapping him over in the evenings and crying my eyes out, praying, 'Come back safe – please come back safe.' That picture of Beau Bob had stuck in my brain: I could not bear the thought of that happening to Royal Mail.

'My' three horses leaving Linkslade for the 1981 Grand National – *l–r* Pacify, Royal Mail, Royal Stuart.

All three at the 20th fence. Nearest – Royal Stuart with Hwyel Davies about to fall with a broken leather. Centre – Pacify with Steve Jobar who would fall two fences later. Far side – Royal Mail and Philip Blacker who would be third to Aldaniti and Bob Champion. Number 10 is Rubstic.

In the 1981 National, Royal Mail was third to Bob Champion and Aldaniti, and I did not only have him in the race, I also had the other two horses I was at doing at the time: Royal Stuart and Pacify. Royal Stuart was in the next-door box to Royal Mail, and was also a chestnut up from New Zealand. They were quite similar to look at, but Royal Stuart was a bit darker, and a longer, heavier horse. Royal Stuart was quite decent, though: he had been third in the Hennessy the previous season, and in 1981 was going well when he and Pacify and Royal Mail all jumped the 20th fence together – Stan has got a picture of it: three stablemates side-by-side on the second circuit of the National, and all looked after by the same lad. Bet that has never happened before or since. Trouble was, while Royal Mail kept on and was third, just after Jobi yelled, 'Going better than you' at Philip, Pacify fell at Becher's, and as for Royal Stuart, immediately after that photo was taken he turned over because Hwyel Davies' stirrup leather had broken as he landed.

The next year Royal Mail was favourite – imagine that: Grand National favourite! All the press and TV came down – he was in the papers every day. The thought of it became quite a pressure on me, what with the threat of somebody trying to nobble him. On the Thursday night before we were due to drive up to Liverpool I actually slept in the box with him and Jenny the donkey he had inherited from Pacify. When we were all inside, my brother Chrissie parked my car hard against the door so nobody could break in.

It was quite a trip for Chrissie, who had never been to anything like this before. When he turned up at Stan Mellor's he was in jeans, and I told him he could not go to the Grand National in jeans, so when we got to Aintree we went out and bought him some trousers, only to have them stolen by someone in the hostel that night and have to buy another pair next day. Royal Mail had been given top weight of twelve stone to carry in that National, and in the weeks before, Philip and I used to joke as we rode home from the gallops in the mornings that he really would have a much, much better chance if I could somehow slip the weight cloth under my mac so he'd then carry only 11 stone. Of course, Philip denies it all now – don't forget he is a member of the Jockey Club as well as a famous sculptor – but I remember us talking about it, and I had a good idea how I could do it quick enough for nobody to notice!

Anyway, Philip messed it all up by getting laid out in a Novice Chase at Aintree on the Friday. So Bob Davies rode Royal Mail: they fell at Becher's, and I then had one of my worst moments in racing as I ran out on to the National course hoping and praying that my horse was not dead or injured. I ran down the track with loose horses galloping past, but Royal Mail was not among them. I was crying – I could not bear it. But then – there he was.

Royal Mail retired at the end of the season, and so did Philip. I had hoped I could somehow keep Royal Mail as a hack, but they gave him to Philip and he practised his sculpture on him. The extraordinary thing about the horse is that he never, ever, whinnied: not a blow of the nostrils, not anything. He never whinnied until the day he died. Philip told me that that day he suddenly heard Royal Mail whinny, and when he looked out the horse had dropped dead in the field.

It was good to have Chris come to Aintree, but things remained pretty difficult with my family. Despite everything Reg and Tom were still around and even though Tom became a church minister near Oxford, he then got caught molesting choir boys, the headline said one of them in the pulpit, and he was sent to jail in April 1984. I remember being in the car with my father driving and my mother reading out an article in the *Sun* about Tom being jailed and so many 'other cases being taken into account'. She sort of laughed at it – called him 'Tom the Hom'. Believe it or not, when my brother Kevin got married in September 1981, Reg was his best man. Reg can't have messed around with Kevin, but he had with the rest of us, although we had not told each other at that stage. Then another day I went down to Poole to see my mother, and was walking up the road with her when we saw Tom going into a shop on the other side. Straight away she went over to say hello to him – Tom 'the Hom', the man she knew had abused me. I could not believe it; I just walked away. I may have had horses to look after, but what I really needed was a family of my own.

'Hipparion was great and took me all over the place, winning on the flat as well as over hurdles.'

05 | Growing Confidence

Reg and Gill Dixon still live in Lambourn, their small terraced house hardly a mile from the hostel they ran for Stan and Elain Mellor in the 1970s and 1980s. Stan always referred to Reg Dixon as 'Borneo Bill' because of his Aussie drover's hat; Elain remembers Gill as 'a very warm, loving, motherly person, much too nice to be a cook in a lads' hostel! And there was this pretty little eldest daughter called Julie. It was the family that Gary had never had.' 'Oh, yes, he was a nice quiet boy back then,' says Gill Dixon with a smile.

The Dixons have seen plenty, put up with a lot, and can still smile at the memories. One of those was how Gary Witheford came to court and marry Julie. Gill was a Baptist, even if Reg Dixon was a more moderate churchgoer, and whether, in view of Gary's later trouble and divorce, his courtship of their daughter was wholly welcome is an unfair question. But there was no doubting that the still quite shy 'Shylock' of the inventive schemes and the big ideas about horses had an energy about him. 'Oh, yes,' says Reg Dixon: 'Gary had ideas all right, and he and Julie were very happy for a while. But I suppose it all became too difficult for him.'

Gary remains pretty high-maintenance to this day, and it's not hard to imagine the hassle that Julie went through. The two young people may have been well matched by location, but while Gary was obsessed with animals in general and horses in particular, Julie was not an animal lover. She tolerated Sheba until she and Gary finally married in July 1983, but after that it was outside in the kennel. Her husband was to change jobs, but he could not change his interests. He may have craved a family, but present circumstances combined with past history would always create trouble for him. It became clear then, and remains so now, that he deals much better with animals than with people.

There would be some stormy scenes before Gary finally led Julie down the aisle in St Michael and All Angels in Lambourn, with Sheba on hand for the wedding photos. On his 21st birthday he managed to provoke such a family quarrel that he stormed out and walked home through a snowstorm. But an increasing mastery of his own equine language meant there were good times too. None better than when he took on the bookies at Sandown...

Nobody rode Royal Pine bar me, because nobody wanted to. They all thought he was a horrible, skanky-looking thing – which he was. He was a big, green, strapping 17-hand horse always going a bit lame, dancing around at exercise. By complete coincidence, as he had not come from anywhere near New Zealand, he was in the corner box next to Royal Mail and Royal Stuart. He was owned by Bill Whitbread, who had good horses. But no one rated this one. Philip Blacker certainly didn't. Mind you, he was biased, because his parents had bought Royal Pine's dam, very much against his advice. He had ridden her and hated her, and could not believe that anything she produced could be any good. So when he saw me on this big thing, sweating and jig-jogging every morning, it just confirmed what he wanted to think.

I rode Royal Pine for a year, a whole year, and I got to understand him. Of course he was difficult, and you could not take him with other horses, but I realised that he could gallop – yes, he could really go. Philip and I used to talk a lot as we rode through Mandown Bottom back to the yard. I began to tell him that this was a nice horse – 'I promise you, Philip, a real nice horse.' He wouldn't have it: 'Oh, yeah, yeah' – he was never going to be convinced. Not until Royal Pine ran for the first time – at Doncaster.

It was a grisly day and nobody was there: it must have been at the end of December 1980. Philip rode him and he got badly impeded, had to sidestep, lost all his momentum, and still finished fifth. To this day I can remember Philip coming back in: he had snot all over his face and was blowing a little as jockeys do at the end of a race. As I ran up to him he looked at me, eyes blazing, and said, 'Don't say anything – don't say anything to anyone. We'll have this off – keep your mouth shut. Keep your mouth shut!'

Royal Pine went to Sandown three weeks later and p***** up. I had the biggest gamble I ever had on a horse. I had been to Stan and got out my holiday money; I used my pool money; I borrowed money. I got other people to back it: my Uncle Billy, the one who had backed Baltic Love – he went round Wolverhampton backing it. When I got to the races I had another £50 on. They backed it from 8s into 3s, but I mostly got the big prices. I must have had £300 on – and don't forget I was on a tenner a week. My, I won some money! I went off and bought myself my first car: a green Triumph Dolomite Sprint with spoke wheels and a black vinyl roof. It could do 120 mph. It was a bloody smart car to look at – even though it turned out to be a pain in the **** – and I thought I was a million dollars.

Reg and Gill Dixon's house at Stan Mellor's. It became a second home for me.

Royal Pine taught me not to give up too quickly on a horse, and I was beginning to sense that I could do things with them. Other horses did too. One day we had to send a horse up to Nottingham and it would not go into the horse box. They had the back ramp down on the bank to make it easier. They pushed it, pulled it and beat it, but it absolutely would not load. So in the end I just said, 'Leave it to me.' I must have spent an hour with it, but I remember trying to imagine how it was thinking. I thought it must be frightened going up into that little cramped hole, which was what the partition in the horse box would look like to him. He didn't know it would actually be quite comfortable: it just looked like a poky little cell. So I went first: I walked up and messed around up there. I thought he wanted me to lead him, not pull him or drive him. It took a long time, but in the end he followed me. Without me realising how it would become central to all my theory on Natural Horsemanship he had accepted me as his leader. Let the horse bang the ramp with his feet, sniff the sides to make sure, but always walk ahead yourself. I have never had a problem with loading a horse since.

Then we had another horse that taught me about 'twitches' – you know, those little rope loops they put on a horse's top lip and then tighten until the poor thing is standing rigid to avoid the pain. They are still used all the time today: if something is making the horse jumpy, you either dope it or put a twitch on it. Well, there are some horses that won't take a twitch – like this one. She was a big chestnut mare – I can't remember her name, but I know for a fact she was useless, never won a race. She was a great big 17.2 thing, home-bred and spoilt. And I have still got a hole in my head from what happened to me.

I was going to clip her. Bill Strong, the travelling head lad, used to do the clipping, and he taught me about clipping, and pulling manes, and things like that. I did it for the extra money: £2 for a trace [half] clip, £5 a full clip. That would be matching my wages, and I worked at it so I could trace-clip a horse in ten minutes. The yearlings would come in all woolly with their winter coats, and I would trace-clip them five minutes each side from above the stifle, across the belly and up the neck. That's two quid, thank you very much. I wasn't frightened; I didn't quarrel with them: I just got stuck in. I used to do them on my own – I didn't dope them or twitch them: I just put the pressure quietly on them like I had learned with Baltic Love. Desensitise them, take the 'flight' out of them, so they accept what you want of them.

But with this mare Bill said I would need to twitch her. He said it would be all right: the vet had explained that the pain from the twitch releases endorphins, and so it was a good idea. Well, I have never thought that either doping or twitching was right: if you're doping them you're going to have to face the day when they can't be doped, and somebody's going to get hurt. Then with the twitch, it can only go so far – it's like me holding your nail under pressure: it hurts so much you'll quickly give in. But there might come a point when you just explode. That's what happened with this mare: it went absolutely crazy, and knocked me flat. I came round in the hostel.

Every yard still has twitches. Some of my staff have used them, but I haven't, and I saved two of their lives one day. I said to them, 'Don't put a twitch on that horse,' but they promised me it would be fine. I could see it was about to flip and pulled them both out of the door just as its bomb went off. 'I told you so,' I said. With those sort of horses the twitch builds up pressure to the point where they just explode.

Back at Stan's I was getting my confidence. I was engaged to Julie whose parents, Reg and Gill, looked after the staff hostel; I

The wedding group when Julie and I married in Lambourn on 16th July 1983. Julie's Dad is on the left, mine on the right and Alan Stonell, the best man is next to Julie. How young we all were!

was doing good horses; I was doing all the special jobs. I should have been easier to deal with, but I wasn't. I was impetuous: that row on my 21st birthday was not the only one, and while I did more and more of the chores around the stable, from clipping to loading to lunging, I was riding less work because I was getting heavier. Nothing pisses a lad off more than riding up to the gallops and then being 'jocked-off' by someone else. After Royal Mail retired in April of 1982, I walked out.

I had done it once before, but only briefly. This time lasted all summer. I went and worked down in Poole; I went to Toby Bulgin's for a bit; but deep down I knew I had done the wrong thing, and when I saw Elain Mellor at the races in September she said, 'Why don't you come back?' and so I did. Without realising it, there was something I had started at Stan's that I was missing – something that would change my life. Something that should make everyone with horses change the way they think.

'Mister Lord was good fun. He had a trick too – he used to catch my cap.'

06 | Breaking the Mould

Eric Wheeler was old-school and proud of it. In the 1950s he had been through a five-year apprenticeship at West Ilsley with Jack Colling, a trainer so sure of himself that when told that his landlord Lord Astor had arrived for a look round he said, 'Well, he hasn't got an appointment. I'm off shooting.'

As an apprentice Eric got five shillings a week, the bus fare to Newbury and £12 to kit himself out for a year. Four years after he signed on with Colling, he was sent to do National Service with the King's Troop Royal Horse Artillery in London's St John's Wood, alongside such future racing stalwarts as Barry Hills and Jack Berry. Many adventures were had, but when demobbed Eric was still keen enough to return to West Ilsley to progress up through the ranks and take senior positions under Jack Colling and his successor Dick Hern.

A parting of the ways led him to take a year out working at furniture removal in his home town of Poole in Dorset. But when Stan Mellor set up training, it was Eric Wheeler he sought out, with the simple maxim, 'You run the yard and I'll fill the boxes.' The new-broom trainer proved as good as his word.

'We had a lot of good horses,' says Eric, 'so there was plenty for a young lad like Gary to do. His family were living down in Poole as mine were, but I don't think there was any favouritism in the horses I allocated to him. He was just another kid who seemed keen but

looked too heavy to make a jockey. I told him to stick with me and I could make him into a very good head lad one day.

'I didn't really notice anything much to start with. I don't think all the things he does now came to the fore until after he had gone to see Monty Roberts in America. When he came back he seemed to have got his thinking in order from ideas that had been cooking in there all the time. Gary has a quite different way of thinking about a horse's brain. He obviously learned from Monty Roberts, but then went deeper into it all on his own. He will tell you what a horse is going to do before it does it. I have been with horses all my life and I have never seen anyone like him. Don't think anyone has.

'But back then Gary was just a useful kid who was big and strong and seemed to have a bit of a way with horses. So more and more I used to leave things to him. Especially the "breaking".'

The thing I was most looking forward to when I went back to Stan's was 'breaking' the yearlings. Well, I don't like to use the word 'breaking': I would much rather say 'starting', because that's what you are doing, especially with the younger flat horses. But everyone still uses the word 'breaking', and when our yearlings arrived Eric Wheeler and his team would go into battle. Yes, 'go into battle': that's how we thought about breaking the yearlings. So as I was the guy Eric had come to use for all the odd jobs, when the first bunch of yearlings arrived – it must have been October 1980 – I was taken completely off riding horses to help with breaking.

There would be four or five of us going into the covered school with a little yearling – a little yearling! I'm thinking, 'What's happening?' Don't forget that most of my time in racing had been spent with great big jumpers, usually at least four years old and often much older. Of course, I had been at Beckhampton for a while, but even those horses were at least two years old. Now these things were coming in as little babies, everything whinny, whinny, whinny, 'What's it all about?' They were coming to a new place from the sales ring, or from the studs if they were home-breds. I remember bringing this first horse in and there were four, five, might even have been six people there, all holding on to it with a Cavesson head collar and a lunge rein while somebody put a pad on its back and then buckled a roller round it. I was just a young lad who hadn't seen all this before, but I was thinking, 'What's going on?' Then somebody picked up a Long Tom, shooed the horse off, and went *crack, crack, crack* with the Long Tom. All of a sudden this horse was exploding round the ring – buck, buck, buck. 'Ah, now we're going to break him,' they said, and I'm thinking, 'Poor frigging horse' – for it was sent round and round until it was black with sweat and they thought it was time to bring it in. Then the next minute they lifted its tail, threaded it through a crupper attached to the roller, and sent it off bucking all over again. 'Yeah,' they used to say: 'he'll be fine. Let's buck him out of it.'

First they had put a roller on the little thing, which had made it buck. Then they had beaten him for bucking. Then put a crupper up under his tail which made him buck again – and then they'd beaten him again. He didn't know why he was getting beaten. It was the first yearling I had seen, and when it came in all blowing and worried it was put back in its box with all the tack on to 'get used to it – he'll ****ing get used to it.' And while that yearling was finishing in the school and black with sweat, the next one was watching, waiting for its turn. What was it supposed to think? It was the first time I had ever seen all this, and I remember thinking, 'Poor little babies. There has got to be a better way than this.'

After about a week they put a saddle on, the bucking started all over again, and then the Long Tom came out, *crack, crack, crack*. There was no question of putting anyone on the animal yet, because the idea was that you should long-rein them for weeks to give them 'a mouth' before they could be ridden: you would walk behind them and drive them up the road – it was crazy, crazy, crazy. One day a horse called Mummy's Star backed up and kicked me in the face. It knocked me clean out, and because we were taught to have the end of the long reins looped around round our wrists, it dragged me behind it as it galloped straight back to its box. It skinned me nearly all over, and the only reason people knew about it was because the horse galloped straight past the hostel as the other lads were finishing their breakfast.

That first year of breaking I just went along with the system. After all, this was what happened everywhere, and anyway Saxon Farm and Tenth Of October, two of the horses we 'broke', turned out really decent, and were later to be first and second in the 1983 Triumph Hurdle. But Eric realised I was interested: I thought, 'I could do this,' and so he said, 'OK – get on with it,' and gradually it got to a stage where I was enjoying doing it without anybody around. And I worked out that you didn't actually have to do all these things and take so much time: the young horse learns quickly, especially if he trusts you. Why did you have to put a roller on? Why don't you just put a saddle on straight away? After all, it's going to have a saddle on for the rest of its life. But rather than start by putting the saddle on in all the fuss in the school, I would do it quietly in its own box.

And then there was the Cavesson. This is the noseband to which you attach the lunge reins. To begin with there is no bit in the horse's mouth, so the reins are buckled to rings on the noseband, and what happens is that the rings squeeze the cartilage on the nose. It's a nutcracker on the nose: that's how it works, and these horses – they're really babies – are fighting it. That's what makes it so bloody cruel. People use it, but I never have. I had one in the yard, but I've thrown it out.

The whole process of breaking was about people holding on and waiting for these animals to take off. But if you do it my way the horse starts to learn that actually it's got nothing to fear. Instead of everyone hanging on to the horse waiting for it to explode, it actually starts to learn. That word 'break' is a horrible word, so from the second year I began a mission to see if I could 'start' the horses not in six weeks, but in less than a month. I began to get them done in a week, and then I had it down to three days. Nowadays I can get them started, backed and ridden away in thirty minutes. But of course it is only a 'start'. It is still going to take time before they really understand what is wanted, and you need to be riding them in a controlled environment for a while – not going out onto the road or even into a big field. But the point is that most horses, especially the young horses, want to learn. What's more, they are first-time learners. Once they have done something, they remember. That's why it's so important to start out in a sensible way and not have all this drama. Horses forgive, but they never forget.

In many ways what I had done – getting the 'breaking' down from six weeks to three days – was a huge breakthrough. But no one seemed to notice very much: they just left me to get on with it. Eric was happy for me to do my thing, and Stan and Elain must have been impressed, because a few years later they would recommend me as someone to go and visit the 'Horse Whisperer' Monty Roberts in California, and that would change my life. Back then I was just a young lad in the yard: a lot of people didn't believe in this natural horseman thing, and quite a few still don't today. They still say a horse has to have all that driving in long reins to give it a 'mouth', when all that old-fashioned stuff is a myth. It's the hardest thing to change their minds. They need to see it to believe it.

In that second batch of yearlings there were four home-breds from a stud in Yorkshire. They were all colts, and all by Gunner B, a chestnut horse who had won the Eclipse and a lot of other good races for Henry Cecil. There was Son Of A Gunner, Star Of A Gunner, Love Of A Gunner and Gold Of A Gunner. I 'started' them all off, and when I took one of the colts away, the other three started screaming and shouting: they wanted to be together because they were herd animals. So when I was working the first one in the school, I would get the lads to lead the other Gunners outside and let them look in to see how their mate was getting on.

They all turned out all right, and Son Of A Gunner became one of the horses I did. He was a gorgeous-looking colt, not very big but powerful, and he had a fantastic coat that didn't need clipping even in winter. He was absolutely full of character – if he had been a man he would have been Arthur Daley: I'm sure he would have made a great jumping stallion. His party trick was rolling in the shavings just after I had finished making him spick-and-span. Every evening at half past five Stan would come round to feel each horse's legs. I would have just spent an hour dressing Son Of A Gunner over, putting quarter-marks on his backside, damping down his mane, greasing his feet and making him look perfect. Then when the bastard heard the old man he would slip his head collar off and get down and roll and come up covered in shavings. Every single night. He was a swine, he was.

I tried everything. I tried tightening the rope up short, then two ropes, but somehow he would still pull back and wriggle out of the head collar, have his roll and then stand there smiling at me afterwards. What made it difficult is that Mister Lord, the other horse I did at the time, was just two boxes away. So I had to show Mister Lord to Stan and then run round to Son Of A Gunner while the old man was in the next box. Every night as I got round to him there was Gunner climbing off the floor. He was Houdini.

Mister Lord was a big black colt who belonged to Simon Tindall, one of our best owners, and apparently had won a decent race in Ireland. But when we tried him on the gallops he could not get out of his own way. 'Guvnor,' Eric said to Stan, 'you better have a ride on this – I think you've bought a wrong 'un, because this thing can't go.' So Stanley rode him, and got off afterwards and said, 'I think you're right, Eric: he isn't worth two bob, is he?' I remember they delayed and delayed running Mister Lord, because they were worried about how badly he might do. But when he finally went to Newbury he ran so well that the jockey, Mark Perrett, said he should have been in the Triumph Hurdle. Mister Lord turned out a real good horse for me. He won over hurdles and was even better on the flat. Elain Mellor won races on him which helped make her champion lady rider, and he won a good race at Goodwood under Michael Wigham.

Mister Lord was very 'mouthy', like some colts are, but he taught me that the more mouthy colts get, the more you can tame them. Some people used to hate them chewing at things and would chain them up. If they got 'colty' and started waving their penises around, they would slip on a rubber ring which pinches if the colt gets aroused. It's a horrible thing, because you need to take it off and wash it every day, and I know of one horse who went savage because the lad left the ring on and it got embedded into the flesh – ouch! But being 'mouthy' is what colts are, and Mister Lord was good fun. He had a trick, too: he used to catch my cap. I used to throw it at him and he would catch it and throw it back to me. I would win money off the other lads at the races by betting them I could do it. My father even came to the stables and I showed him – he thought it was a laugh.

Simon Tindall was a great owner: he was always pleased to see you, and would give you a drink every time. That's how we rated owners. Chris Glynn, the owner of Pacify, was the best: £10 every time he saw you, and £50 for a winner – and me on £10 a week! You can see how we liked it. Son Of A Gunner's owner was special too: he was Desmond Morris, who had written *The Naked Ape*, and was on TV all the time doing zoo programmes. Son of a Gunner was the first horse he had ever had – I think he had really bought it for his son Jason, who had won a scholarship and was racing mad. Desmond and his wife were

With Son Of A Gunner and his owner Dr Desmond Morris.

lovely people, and when Julie and I got married they sent us £100 as a wedding present.

Son Of A Gunner was very quick, and the only horse I know who won a five-furlong sprint first time out as a three-year-old, and then went on to win four novice hurdles over two miles in the autumn. That first time on the flat was at Warwick in April and the day before my car had broken down coming out of the petrol station. The Triumph Dolomite had gone by then and I had this Cortina that often wouldn't start, but the guy in the petrol station came out and said, 'Don't worry – take my car: I don't need it.' I was so grateful that I told him to back Son of a Gunner the next day. The horse hosed up at 10-1, and then the guy from the garage kept ringing up, asking, 'Got any more?'

Obviously, if Son Of A Gunner was fast enough to win over five furlongs, he would need to learn a different rhythm if he was to be any good over two miles over hurdles. He had to learn to settle, so I rode him away on his own a lot, to *relax, relax, relax*. When he did run he almost settled too much: at Chepstow when Jimmy Nolan rode him he dropped him right out and they were still stone last coming to the second last. I think Jimmy panicked a bit, because he picked his stick up and gave Gunner an almighty whack over the backside, and the horse sprinted through and beat one of Jenny Pitman's that they thought a lot of. Mrs Pitman didn't look at all pleased.

Gunner was very good to me. He won me five in all, and was fifth at the 1984 Cheltenham Festival – the first English horse home in an Irish-first-four Triumph Hurdle. He was going to have one more run at Ascot before going to stud as a jumping stallion, but then one morning he slipped up on the road turning round opposite Seven Barrows – he had flinched when the horse in front swished its tail, and the guy on board smacked him, which he shouldn't have done. Gunner was a very kind horse, but he jumped from the whip and slipped up, and snapped his hind leg.

I was in the school 'backing' a two-year-old – I was actually leaning across its back when this Australian guy gallops up and runs in to me shouting, 'Gary, Gary – your horse, your horse! It's bad, bad.' The Australian was quite a tough bloke but he was absolutely distraught. We tied his horse up and jumped in the yard car, and I remember driving down and finding Son Of A Gunner on the floor. He had broken his hock: there was blood on the road, there wasn't much skin holding the leg together, and he was thrashing around with this idiot smacking him to try and get him to stand up.

I jumped out of the car and said, 'What the **** are you doing?' I sat on Gunner's head and talked to him: he just lay still, poor old monkey. The Aussie raced back to call the vet, and it seemed a lifetime looking at this horse with its leg split and blood pumping out on to the road. Then the vet came, had one look at Gunner and took the gun out and shot him. When he died it nearly finished me.

'Cozy Powell might have been a rock star and me an ex-stable lad but he became my best mate.'

07 | The Wrong Road

Dr Desmond Morris' bones may be getting as old as any near-nonagenarian's are entitled to be, but his mind isn't frail at all. After producing more than 50 books, 500 television programmes and 2,000 mostly surrealistic paintings, his conversation remains just as sharp and engaging as when he was a polymathic zoologist on our TV screens in the 1970s and 1980s.

His book The Naked Ape *was the publishing sensation of 1967, running to nine editions and 23 languages, and managing to get itself banned by schools as anti-Christian. Maybe, but a more likely reason for the ban was the book's contention that man 'is the sexiest primate alive', and the brilliantly provocative statement about 'homo sapiens' in its opening paragraph. 'He is,' wrote the future owner of Son Of A Gunner, 'proud that he has the biggest brain of all the primates, but attempts to conceal the fact that he also has the biggest penis, preferring to accord this honour falsely to the mighty gorilla.'*

Such an active mind was always going to be fascinated by the daily battles of hope against experience that define the racing world, and by the two- and four-legged creatures that inhabit it. 'We didn't know much about it, but Jason was very keen,' says Morris of his son, who is now a major player at Horse Racing Ireland as Director of Racing. 'But we had a wonderful time. Son Of A Gunner was such a tremendous horse, and my wife Ramona always said how calm he and Gary seemed together. She spotted that. She said, "There is something special about this boy." And of course, we were all absolutely shattered when Gunner got killed.'

The effect on the Morris family was to put them off racehorse ownership, even if the better parts of the experience helped with Dr Morris' 1988 book Horsewatching, *which included the assertion (not accepted by G. Witheford) that horses don't know whether they are winning or even in a race – 'to them it is simply an exercise combined with something resembling herd panic'. But the impact of Son Of A Gunner's demise on the young man who had cradled the horse's head until the final moments was more fundamental. It deepened his disillusionment with the life, and in particular the pay, of a stable lad, and in June 1985 he went to work for Marley Tiles near Thatcham for ten times the money.*

On the face of it, this was a no-brainer: Gary and Julie had been married in July of 1983, and Gemma Louise Witheford had been born the following August. Now they could afford to move into their own little home in Child Street, Lambourn, and with regular hours and weekends the set-up should have been better for both of them.

But the world, particularly for those caught up in the horse world, doesn't work like that. Gary was supposed to have left the game, but in his heart he couldn't. His dream would never die, even when the rest of his life would descend into the darkest of nightmares.

She and I would go off on our own. We would wander for hours out along the Ridgeway. She had been very wound up, and it settled her down. Mind you, by then I needed settling, too.

She was called Forest Fawn. She was French-bred, but hadn't shown a lot until she ran second in a claiming hurdle on the all-weather at Lingfield – they still had all-weather racing over jumps in those days. As it was a claiming hurdle Eric Wheeler put in a bid and claimed her. From 1988 Eric had rented Stan's top yard and was training on his own. But when he got Forest Fawn home she was very jazzed-up. She was quite big, almost black, but so restless that she was as lean as a hat rack. So I rode her.

She didn't come to Eric's until December 1989. It was almost five years since I had finished with stables, but I had never really stopped riding out. If I was working a night shift I would finish at six in the morning and get back to Lambourn for first lot at seven. On a day shift I would get back and take one out later in the afternoon. I wasn't paid for it, but I couldn't leave horses – I felt I had to keep my hand in. I always thought I would end up with horses.

But life should have been much better. When I left Stan's I got a mortgage on my Marley Tiles pay and moved into this little house in Child Street just off the Baydon Road. I was 25, Julie 21, and Gemma nearly one. It was our first home: a typical Charles Church 'new-build', one of a group of four with two bedrooms, a little box-room third bedroom, and a small garden out the back. It cost £30,000, it was terrific, and at Marley Tiles I could earn good money to get the mortgage off my back.

I work hard to this day, but I have never worked as hard as I did then. Marley Tiles were at Beenham, just the other side of Thatcham, and I started on the production line making these roof tiles. Marley were very happy to pay overtime, so I would get up at 4 a.m., and get in at quarter to five to clean the line ahead of the 6 o'clock shift. At the end of that I would go on to the 2 p.m. lot and do another half-shift with them. If I was working nights I would get home at 7 a.m. on Saturday morning, have a sleep, and then go back at 4 a.m. on Sunday and work all day on overtime. From earning something like under £30 a week in racing I was bringing back £500 a week or more. It was unbelievable money, and we should have been paying off the mortgage as quick as we could. But it actually became more difficult. Craig was born in 1986, and Callie in 1989, and in between we moved out of Child Street to Braythorn House just opposite Brown and Warren's in Station Road. It was a bigger house with a better garden, but it meant a heavier mortgage. You can't rewind the clock, but it would probably have been better if we had stayed in Child Street.

Within six weeks of going to Marley Tiles I had been promoted to charge hand – one below the foreman and a big step-up for someone of my age. After Craig was born Julie started playing tennis again: she had been a County player at school. Although I had never played much, I became quite good too – three years running I was in the semi-final of the handicap singles, and one year I only lost in the final to Kevin Mooney, who is now Head Lad for Charlie Hills and as a jockey won the Whitbread for the Queen Mother. For £50 Julie and I became life members of the Lambourn Sports Club, but I did find it very cliquey.

I preferred to do motocross down in Poole with my brother Chrissie, with our dad as 'pitman'. They used to call me 'Gary Gearbox', because they could hear me crashing the gears as I went round. When you get used to it, the sound of the engine automatically changes the gear for you, but while I had ridden a bike I had never done a cross-country course before. I found there was a lot of difference between pulling a rein and handling a gear lever – the bike would be literally running away with me. The first race I did had something like 20 laps of a track which had a river at its lowest point. I must have got stuck in that river every time: I would crash the gears and rock over – I can remember my father sitting on the bank just wetting himself laughing. He would change the rings and pistons on my bike and help me to keep going. But it was expensive: you could rip a tyre in two or three rides, and money was getting difficult. So was everything.

After a couple of years at Marley Tiles, the guy who used to drive the fork-lift trucks told me that I ought to join him at the Thermalite factory nearer the centre of Thatcham – he had recommended me. I went for an interview and got the job. At the time it was the most modern production line in the country. We worked continental shifts – two days on, two days off; two nights on, two nights off. In theory, you could have six months on and six months off. There was £1,500 a month basic, masses of overtime, and I could still ride out at Eric's or Stan's. It should have worked out nicely, but if someone called in sick you had to do a cover shift. You always felt as if you were jet-lagged, so you had no social life at all. Then the recession came. Mortgages went through the roof. Instead of £400 I was paying £900 a month. It couldn't hold.

Anyway, Julie and I were having trouble. We had been 16 and 13 years old when we first met, and Reg and Gill Dixon had been like second parents to me. I had loved Julie to bits. Our wedding had been the happiest day of my life. Her mum and dad and my mum and dad and all our friends had been there; Alan Stonell was best man, and Sheba was the guest of honour – have a look at the photos. But we were growing apart. We already had two children, and Callie was to come in September 1989, and before then Craig was in hospital three times for a cyst that kept growing in his throat. It would get to the size of an apple, and then they would cut it out. He would be in for about four days each time, and I would sleep in a chair beside his bed. It was very upsetting – he has scars on his throat to this day. I was working all sorts of hours to pay the mortgage and then, if possible, riding out, which Julie could not understand. We began to quarrel – about money, about everything. Sheba dying didn't help me. She had been my best friend for eleven years, but got a twisted gut one evening and died very quickly. I got another sheepdog, but she was not a Sheba and I ended up giving her away. Eventually we got a terrier puppy we called Snoopy: Julie had chosen her and they got on well together.

When the recession hit, Thermalite had to lay off a lot of people. They said, 'Good news, Gary – we want you to stay.

You can keep your job.' But I told them I wanted voluntary redundancy: I was going to take the money and set up with my friend Dave Bosher in his window-fitting business. Both Dave's knees were shot and he could not do ladder work any more. The idea was that I would go in with him, fit the windows and do odd jobs and labouring and the rest of his building work. Dave and I got on and it kept me busy, but the mortgage people were getting on my back: they were talking about repossession and I was getting desperate. A guy called Craig Pilgrim set up as an estate agent in Lambourn and we got some housing work from him. I met some nice people. One of them was Cozy Powell.

Cozy was a rock legend. He had been a drummer with Ozzy Osbourne in Black Sabbath. He was still working with all sorts of big names and touring with Brian May. From the outside he could be a real 'rocker', with a bike and a leather jacket and letters and photos from birds that would make your hair curl. But at heart he was quiet and quite shy like I was. He loved the country. He owned a place called Bold Start Farm above Lambourn, opposite Kingwood Stud. One spring the cottage got flooded, and Craig Pilgrim sent me up to clear it. Cozy came round and started chatting. We got on: he'd been a Barnardo's Boy, so he'd had family trouble, too. I think we got on because I never asked him for tickets or anything like his hangers-on all did. He listened to me talk about horses – he had broken his pelvis falling off his own horse the year before. He might have been a rock star and me an ex-stable lad, but he became my best mate.

A couple called John and Sylvia Froome were renting his farm and had horses. They were very good to me and I used to do odd jobs for them; one year I drove them to Royal Ascot for the week. For a while they ran the Ibex pub in Chaddleworth, and I did stints behind the bar. I could talk to them, too – I could tell John about my troubles as a boy, and Sylvia about my difficulties at home. She says now that the only time I really lit up was when I was talking about horses, and that I was so worried about everything I was like a child in a man's body. Sometimes, she says, I seemed in such a state that when I went home she feared I might never come back. She was right: in April my dad died.

It was the day of the void Grand National, 1993, the one that Jenny Pitman won with Esha Ness, but a false start had been called. My dad had driven over with my birthday presents – he had come over by himself, which was unusual because he and my mother usually made the trip together as a day out. They'd had a row or something, but there was another reason: he was worried about the operation he was to have in Southampton Hospital on the Monday to remove a hernia lump on his chest. Five or six years earlier he had had a triple heart bypass, one of the first to be done in Southampton, and this hernia lump was the legacy of it. He had gone back to work after the bypass and been stewarding at the motocross and all that, but when he got home he would be absolutely knackered. My mother didn't like that, but the doctors had told us his heart had been so diseased that what he had left was only the size of a 50p piece. He lost his HGV licence; three times we were told he would not live through the night. He was a tough man.

So on National day Dad and I watched the race together, and I have a picture of him playing 'Horsey' with Callie on his shoulders. We went out into the garden and he helped me with the vegetable patch. Then we took Snoopy for a walk in the woods above Upper Lambourn. Dad knew things were very difficult: that the house might be repossessed, that Julie and I were not getting on. But I remember him saying to me, 'You have got to do what you want to do. The thing you are really good at is horses. You must follow your dream.' Then he drove off home. At the crossroads next to the Five Bells at Wickham a car pulled out without warning, and my dad drove straight into it.

My dad Bill – he told me to follow my dreams.

When I got there he was in the back of the ambulance with monitors on him, and the guys said, 'His heart is very irregular, and we are very worried about him.' They set off down the M4 for Swindon Hospital and I followed in our van. When they got to the first Swindon turning they switched on their flashing blue light. At the hospital they went straight into A&E, and by the time I had parked the car Dad was in the operating room. After what seemed an hour they said, 'You can come and see your father.'

He was in a cubicle with all sorts of tubes in him. He was that grey colour that dying people have. He still had his watch on his wrist – I would have thought they would have taken it off him in the theatre. He took it off and gave it to me and said, 'I won't need this any more.' It was just an ordinary watch, a Seiko, with a leather strap, but I had always joked with him that when he died his watch was the only thing I wanted. Now he gave it to me along with his cigarette lighter and a packet of ten Silk Cut – he was still a secret smoker. They were the only three things he really owned in life. He died at 2.30 the next morning. Some days when I feel really stressed I take that watch out of the drawer and his smell is still there. He was a mechanic, and the smell is that mix of leather, grease and engine oil: his smell.

When we got to the house in Poole before the funeral, who should be in there talking to my mother but Reg Blakeley? Me and all my brothers could not take it, and went and stood outside. Later my mother actually went on holiday with Tom and Reg. I could not understand it. I could not see my way out – I had lost my father; I was about to lose my house, my marriage, my kids. Over the next few days I began to think of putting my gun together. It was in three or four pieces, but then I took it and two cartridges down to the garden shed. I remember loading it and putting the muzzle in my mouth.

Then Craig knocked on the door and said, 'What are you doing in there, Dad?' He must have been seven years old.

'If you want a Zebra I will get you one . . .'

08 | Zebra Mania

In 1994 Monty Roberts was about to become the most famous Horse Whisperer in history, even if Gary Witheford had never heard of him. A former rodeo champion from California, and himself the graduate son of a horse trainer, Monty had developed his own method based on an understanding of a horse language he called 'Equus', and featuring a 'Join-Up' between man and horse within minutes of meeting in a ring. Such was his fame within the horse world that the Queen of England had invited him to do a special demonstration at Windsor Castle.

In most people's eyes Monty Roberts' name became inseparably linked to the 'Horse Whisperer' brand, although neither Nicholas Evans' 15-million-copy bestseller of that name, which came out in 1995 a year before Monty's own autobiography, nor Robert Redford's $187 million-grossing film of the Evans novel, were in any way based on Monty himself. In fact, the main inspiration was the remarkable Buck Brannaman, who also doubled for Robert Redford in the film. Back in Berkshire such details meant nothing to Gary as he fought a losing battle to save his marriage and finances with a white van, work in window-fitting and any other job he could turn his hand to. Yet Monty Roberts was to prove his salvation.

For news of Gary's own talents had spread to a Monty Roberts admirer in Britain called Miranda Bruce, and a chance meeting at Thresher's Barn Saddlery saw Miranda give three Monty Roberts videos to the young man she had heard of as a potential protégé. Gary took them up to Bold Start Farm and watched them with Cozy Powell. A fuse was lit. With Miranda Bruce's introduction and Cozy's backing, Gary hotfooted it to Roberts' famed Flag Is Up Farm in Santa Barbara, California. 'When he left,' said the ever-motherly Sylvia Froome, 'he was still that boy in a man's body, but when he came back he was different. He seemed bigger and taller; he walked with a swing in his step. He was still quiet and shy, but he had something he believed in.'

The road from there to opening what would be called Bold Start Stables, featuring 'The Monty Roberts Join-Up Method by Gary Witheford', was never going to be an easy one. But for all his hassles – Braythorn House had been duly repossessed and the family moved at the last minute to council housing in Hungerford – Gary was both inspired and inspirational. The daughter of the former trainer Farnham Maxwell, Sue Bond, was an early believer. She had been a PR Director for Selfridges before she moved out of London, and was willing to give both professional and financial support in the search for somewhere for Gary to set up on his own. A small yard just outside Wootton Bassett was identified, and in November 1995 the venture was launched without too many people noticing.

Within six months Gary was on the national news. But not quite in the way we might have imagined.

He was a lot smaller than any of the horses I had been asked to handle in those first six months at Wootton Bassett. But then Mombassa was not a horse at all. He was a zebra.

To be exact, he was a Chapman's zebra: he and his mate Melvyn came over from Longleat on the day after the May bank holiday. To us they were both three-year-old colts, although in the zebra world they call them stallions. They would only be 12 hands high, but they were wild as ****. When we lowered the ramp they jumped straight out of the horsebox and bolted out of the yard like kangaroos. They went straight through two sets of rails and got to within a hundred yards of the M4. We never caught them, just steered them round the fields back into the yard and into the same box, the pair of them. This was a bit trickier than I had reckoned on.

It had all started in the pub. I had been telling some people that the way we were training and starting horses would work for any animal of flight – that I would love to do it on something wild like a zebra. A journalist called Josie Lewis overheard me and said, 'If you want a zebra I'll get you one.' She contacted Longleat and then Roger Cawley who was the husband of Mary Chipperfield of Chipperfield's Circus, and in less than a week Mombassa and Melvyn were jumping off the wagon.

Next day I thought I would start on them, but they were ****ing crazy. They would come at you – I frigging mean it: they would attack with their mouth, front legs and back legs all at the same time. Twice they jumped out over the box door, and if you got hold of Mombassa, Melvyn would be bloody shouting and screaming. Eventually I got Mombassa into the pen and put a lunge line on him, but when I tried to make him trot round the side he kept turning in and coming at me. He was a bit of an odd shape: this big head, very short neck and absolutely no wither, and he would stand up to you – one of his kicks cut me across the hand.

After about ten minutes I got him going in both directions, and when he had done that a bit I thought we ought to bring him in to the centre and get the saddle onto him as we were doing with the horses. So Nicky, the girl who worked with us, goes and gets the saddle, but when she puts it on the floor Mombassa just attacks it. He dropped on his knees and bit the saddle, and kept stamping on it with his front legs.

Quite a few people had come to watch – there must have been about 20 of them. I could see them thinking, 'This guy isn't going to make it.' So I tried putting a pad on Mombassa, then the saddle, a little light racing saddle, but when I dropped the girth down the off side he kicked the whole thing off. Every time that girth dropped he would kick and, whoosh, the saddle would go flying in the air. I had to think of something. I couldn't reach underneath his belly because he would kick my head in. So I placed him over some binder twine that I attached to the girth on the off side, and then pulled it across underneath him until I could gradually buckle it up on the near side. Actually he took that quite well, and so I started to do my thing. I shooed him away from me, and he just arched his back and ran – didn't buck or kick like you might expect a horse to do: he just ran away from me round the ring. He must have done five or six circuits flat-out, then suddenly stopped dead.

He wouldn't move. He wouldn't go forward. He wouldn't go backwards. He wouldn't turn. He wouldn't do anything else. He sort of shut down. It was as if a lion had got him by the throat. He just sort of said, 'Well, I can't work this out, so whatever you're going to do with me, do it.' So I got a bridle on him – we needed a flash noseband to stop him biting my hand off – and got some reins on to it and then some long reins. Then, amazingly, he started moving. I began to flap the reins behind him and he trotted round quite well. I turned him two or three times and said that was it for the day: tomorrow we would put a jockey on him. 'Well, I can tell you one thing,' said Nicky, who had been there all through this: 'I am not getting on *that*.'

We'd had plenty of hitches with setting up this place already. Even the trip to Monty Roberts hadn't worked out the way it was planned. Cozy had got the tickets, and I flew to Los Angeles and then on to Santa Barbara, but when I got to the farm it was not easy. Although Miranda Bruce had arranged everything I think there had been a falling-out between her and Monty, and it felt as if he was a bit suspicious of me.

I was only there for about three weeks, but I worked my butt off leading horses, riding horses and watching a lot of stuff. Monty did two or three demos while I was there, and it all fell into place. The basis of his 'Join-Up' is what the Indians have been doing with horses for years. You drive the horse away from you in a ring, make it turn by flicking a rope and angling your body ahead of its eye line, and then ease up, backing off and letting it come to you. It's basically Pressure and Release, and when a horse is ready to accept more instruction he will lower his head and lick and chew his lip to show he is listening. Monty was great, but the best thing was that I could understand it. For while I would not have called this 'Join-Up' – I had been doing a lot of these things when I'd been 'starting' Son Of A Gunner and the others at Stan's. What I had done with them was to turn them to face me, step backwards, and then they would walk in towards me. I had been doing a lot of the Monty things without realising it. What Monty did for me was to put it all into place: he lit the spark as to how all this happened.

But the person I learned most from out there was Hector Martinez, Monty's head groom. He was a tiny little Mexican guy of about six and a half stone who worked very hard for very little money. He had been a jockey but was now about forty, and had a son who lived with him. In my eyes he was a terrific horseman – he did all the things Monty did, and we talked and talked. I tried to get inside his head: we used to go out for a drink, and I remember he used to get pissed very quickly. Little jockeys usually do!

When I got back I was really keen to do something on my own, but my life was a mess – how on earth would I get started? I had sold my gun to the local fireman immediately after that time Craig knocked on the garden shed. I went to the local doctor who first wanted to put me into the Priory, but then got me counselling. To be fair, the lady was really good: she came to see me in the house and a lot of things came out – all that stuff about Tom and Reg that I had never been able to speak about before. She must have talked with me for about three months, and I am sure it was helpful. But it still didn't get the mortgage off our back.

The mortgage company kept sending people down with new schemes that just got us deeper in ****. In the end we were repossessed, and right up until the last minute all the council could

Above: My parents' wedding in Wolverhampton 1957. *Left:* My confirmation at St Anthony's Roman Catholic Church, Changi in Singapore. *Below:* Alan Stonell. The school master at Downland School – and my saviour.

I am 15 and cocky – and I am leading up winners!

My brother Kevin's wedding – the 'delightful' Reg was best man.

The four Witheford boys together in October 1983 at my brother Chris' wedding. Left to right me, Rob, Chris and Kevin.

Below: My children, left to right, Gemma, Callie and Craig.

Old Yard Westcourt 19
it was a dump.

New Yard Westcourt 20
we are proud of it.

Below: Sarah Long – he
support and brains save
me without question.

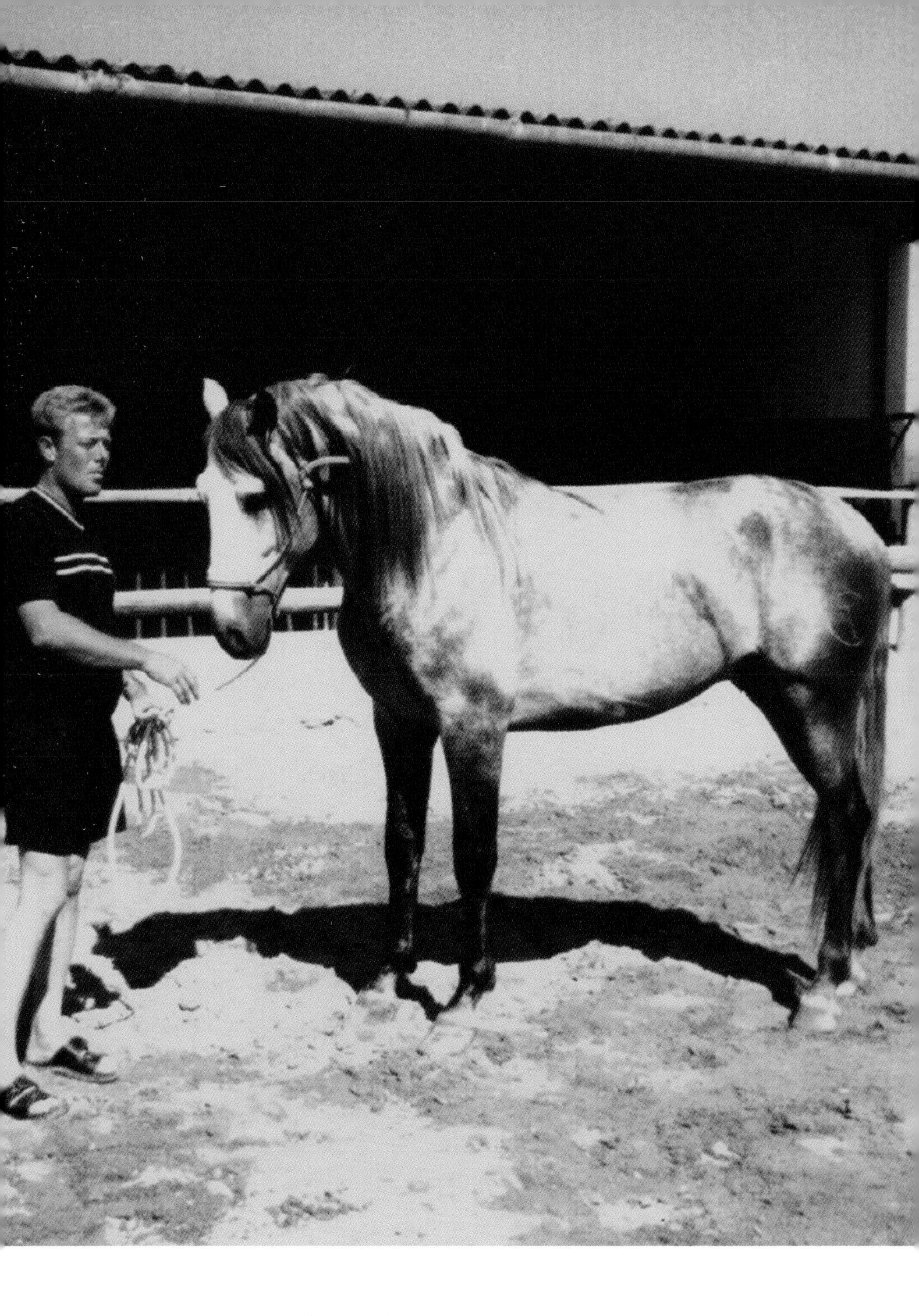

Finding Brujo in Girona – 2002.

Above: Mombassa II, in the snow.

Below: I love seafood. With retired trainer Con Horgan and owner Derek Simester.

Brujo at the Cotswold Show 2009. The jockey is James Doyle – before he was famous!

Mum's 70th birthday with her four sons. Left to right Kevin, me, Chris and Rob.

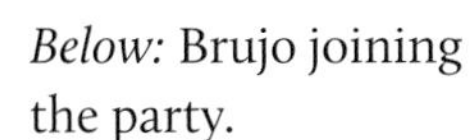

Below: Brujo joining the party.

On cloud nine after Sea The Stars won the Derby. I was so proud.

find us was bed-and-breakfast accommodation in Reading. At the last minute they came up with this house in Hungerford, but I can remember Julie and me sitting in the council office and this guy looking at us as if we were dog dirt, handing us the key and saying, 'Now don't go around saying you own this house, because you don't.' Talk about rubbing our noses in it. We had three children under ten. I was as busy as I could be, but was only doing odd jobs with windows, building work and anything that came up. Julie didn't want to listen to me talking about starting up my own Monty Roberts business. You couldn't blame her.

But others liked it. The Miranda Bruce connection didn't last, but when Cozy Powell was back from tour I would sit with him and talk and talk. The Froomes had noticed how much the trip had excited me, and they had two fillies who were yearlings that I loved handling for them. And a woman called Sue Bond had come over to Lambourn to look after her sick mother, and joined Craig Pilgrim's office as a secretary. I helped her when she and her son moved into a little cottage in Chaddleworth. Her late father was Farnham Maxwell, and she could remember the old-fashioned way of 'breaking-in' yearlings – weeks of long reining and putting sacks of corn on their backs. She had been PR director to some big firms in London, including Selfridges, and she said we ought to look for backers.

Sue Bond was incredible, really – she took me to see all sorts of people. When her mother died, she had to sell the house and things, but she did have a little money. She was prepared to stake me on her own, but first she wanted to see Monty Roberts for herself, and in May of 1995 we both went out to California for ten days. She was really taken by what Monty could do – not just with horses but with people. He would have all sorts of visitors – corporations, big businessmen, Japanese – and he would talk to them as he did his demos. But once again I spent most of my time with Hector. I wanted him to come over to England, and he quite liked the idea, but being Mexican made it all too difficult.

When we got back Sue and I looked at lots of yards, and then in the autumn we found this quite new place we could rent on the Brinkworth Road out of Wootton Bassett. Sue put up £40,000 of her own money and we did a deal. It was owned by Gordon Hunt, who had horses and played polo, and it had eight boxes, an outdoor manège, some decent paddocks and, most importantly, a site where we could place the round pen, which is where all the 'Call-Up' work would happen. Monty had a 50-foot-diameter pen, but mine was 60-foot – I find I can get into their heads better with one this size. The point of these pens is that when you shoo a horse away from you he will naturally 'flight' to the furthest point from you, which is the far side of the pen. In this one we had a good sand base, something called Equiground, and were actually open for business by December. In honour of Cozy Powell's farm, and because the name sounded good, we called it Bold Start Stables.

John and Sylvia Froome sent us our first two horses, the two Nicholas Bill fillies I had seen and handled at Bold Start Farm. They were both three-year-olds, a bay named Bold Start Lady and a chestnut called Arthur. No, I don't know why a filly was called Arthur, either! Bold Start Lady was the first I started in the pen. She was a lovely filly, very kind and loyal: I knew her from the farm, so she was very easy, but the hair still stood up on the back of my neck when she connected up, and I knew that I could make her do what I wanted. The other filly was good, too.

The Froomes also sent us a mare called Puff Puff, who came with a one-horned ram called Barney, who had been everywhere with her and used to gallop beside us when I cantered Puff Puff in the paddock. When the Froomes went to Ireland, the immigration people at first would not allow Barney into Ireland because of the risk of scabies amongst sheep. There was a lot of fuss, and when the pair finally went, the story made the papers.

The word of me being a 'horse whisperer' who could help people with difficult horses had begun to spread, and one of the early ones from outside had been a four-year-old filly who had been running wild on a moor in Cornwall. The journalist Denise Cullimore saw me starting her from scratch to being ridden away in half an hour, and wrote about it in the *Ridgeway Rider*. She also wrote about our other Arthur, which was a 14.2 show-jumping pony that had been banned from several showgrounds for bad behaviour. We took him back to basics and did the same with Richard Haines, the kid who rode him, and when they got back home they were placed in two classes in their first show. Then in May I was talking in the pub and you know what followed with the zebras . . . Well, at this stage you don't know the half of it.

To start with, Josie Lewis had Sky TV coming up to film Mombassa in a couple of days' time, and if our Nicky was not going to ride him, who would? And don't forget, whoever it was had to be very small. Someone told me about this girl called Nicky Davies, who worked in the Cheltenham and Gloucester Building Society and was small enough to ride her own 12.2 pony. I rang her up and said we were starting a pony on TV, and would she like to ride it. Next evening she came over all dressed up, Sue Bond met her and said, 'Gary will show you your ride over there.' So she walked over to the box, opened the top door, and there inside – were the two zebras.

Fair do's to Nicky: she was still game! I took Mombassa over to the ring and lunged him either way. He would not go any faster than a trot, but he did go both ways. Then I went to put

Nicky Davies on Mombassa, the first zebra. He was quite a challenge.

Nicky on him. She only lay across him, but he hated that and – **** me, whoa! – he threw her straight off against the fence. I thought he was probably reacting as if a lion was lying across his neck, and that Nicky would be better off being put straight in the saddle. And he went OK, walking and trotting around: the only thing she couldn't do was touch his side or shoulder with her legs – he hated that, and if she ever did it he would stop and turn round and try and bite her. After half an hour Nicky was riding him loose, and I thought I could do a lot with him.

But he and Melvyn had to go back the next week, and Sky TV were coming the next day. So we did the same thing for the cameras, and he was very good, but you could see he was getting angry – he would swish his tail. At the end they took us out on to the road, on which they had painted white marks, so they could

Nikki's ride on the wild side

Western Daily Press Reporter

STABLE owner Nikki Davies achieved her ambition yesterday when she rode out on a zebra.

The 23-year-old from Swindon has just jumped on three-year-old Mombassa for first time.

She said: "I looked on the idea as a challenge and had a wonderful sense of achievement the first time I sat on his back."

Humans

Owner Gary Witherford from nearby Bold Start Stables, Wootton Bassett, said: "She was on the zebra within 30 minutes.

"I was told zebras were

Challenge changes stripes into a star ride

My kingdom for a zebra?

have pictures saying, 'Zebra Crossing'. Mombassa was beginning to swish his tail a lot by then, but we just about got away with it.

The pictures went everywhere: Sky, Central, HTV. The papers all carried the story, even *The Times*. They said it was the first time a zebra had ever been ridden, and all sorts of PR people and agents started ringing saying they wanted to sign us up. It was all getting a bit silly – we got a call from *The Big Breakfast*: could the zebra come into the studio tomorrow? I said, 'Look, that's it – I've done what we set out to do,' and looking back it was a PR coup beyond everyone's wildest dreams. I was on TV and in all the papers, people were asking me to join them – it should have made life easier. But it didn't.

'It's not something you expect in the middle of the English countryside.'

09 | David and Goliath

Nicky Davies looks back with pride and amusement. For three days she had been a national celebrity: her face (and Mombassa's) had been all over the TV and across the papers. On Friday 24 May the Swindon Messenger *dipped deep into the purple: 'Hannibal rode an elephant,' it intoned, 'Lawrence of Arabia rode a camel, Jesus rode a donkey, but for the first time in history a wild zebra was ridden by a Wiltshire woman on Monday.' The woman in question smiles at the memory: 'I had my five minutes of fame.'*

Nicky is a very small person – not even five foot – and still cannot weigh much more than the six-and-half-stone 23-year-old loaded so effortlessly on to Mombassa's back by Gary that summer of 1996. Nicky is still a frequent presence at the stables, as she was for fifteen years after being whisked from her cashier's desk in Swindon to do zebra duty at Wootton Bassett. 'To start with I just used to come up in the evenings and at weekends,' she says. 'I knew I had to make myself a better rider before I could join full-time. Then almost as soon as that happened we had to leave the stables, with the owner refusing to pay and trying to stop us taking the horses away. It's been a madhouse at times.'

Over the years she has seen a few candidates for the funny farm, both on two legs and on four, as Gary's growing reputation for dealing with equine basket-cases was only matched by the seemingly endless and sometimes self-inflicted traumas in his private and professional life. His first arrangement with Sue Bond was dropped for what appeared a bigger and better offer on the other side of Wootton Bassett. When that ended Gary moved to his present, at that stage very dilapidated, base in a disused dairy farm at Westcourt, six miles south of Marlborough. That arrangement also soured quickly, as the new backers backed-out within the year.

At the same time the Witheford marriage, engulfed in a widening split within the family, had seen the now-teenage Craig opting to go with Gary, while older sister Gemma made it clear she wished to have no contact with her father during this difficult time. Meanwhile, the newly-single Gary became a magnet not just for problem horses but for too-quickly-smitten lady owners who fancied a bit of remedial treatment themselves.

'It was always the same,' sighs Nicky. 'I could read the signs. On the second day they would arrive all made-up and try and befriend me, to get closer to Gary. Back then he was quiet and shy and hardly spoke. I remember he found the public speaking such a strain that during his first demonstration at Wadswick he switched the microphone off. But what he did and still does with horses was extraordinary. I just found it mesmerising.'

Once she had seen Gary Witheford in action, Nicky Davies knew she would be coming back. Trouble was, so would the zebras.

One zebra is not the same as another. Masai was very different from Mombassa and Melvyn. He was quite a bit smaller for a start: he can hardly have been 11 hands. He was actually more affectionate – later on he used to follow me around like a dog. But he was not as easy to ride. He nearly did for me – and for himself, poor little bastard.

It was six months after the Mombassa and Melvyn episode, and I had now moved to the new yard. Masai had come from Mary Chipperfield: he was a yearling, had been on a farm in Devon, and been handled even less than the first two. The idea was to show again that any wild flight animal could be tamed and ridden using my 'Call-Up' method: Meridian TV were behind the project, and wanted to film it from the beginning, but I sensed from the start that something wasn't right – even the presenter was coming at things from a different angle.

They were with us for about three hours. We led Masai about, took him into our round pen, got him turning on the lunge, got the bridle and saddle on him, and Nicky rode him around. He would only walk, but he was fine. Afterwards I sat in the corner of his box and we brought him back, completely relaxed, not a sweat mark on him, and he came in, walked round two or three times, and then lay down and put his head in my lap. And do you know: Meridian TV never showed that.

Protesters hit out over zebra training

By Staff Reporter

A WOOTTON Bassett horse trainer is at the centre of a row over his pioneering efforts to train zebras.

Gary Witheford, 36, has received a string of calls from animal lovers after he was shown on television training one of the zebras.

In the Meridian news piece, the zebra was seen to rear up and fall over in front of the camera, but was uninjured.

The programme suggested the zebra would end up performing in a circus and showed an interview with an outraged animal rights campaigner.

Mr Witheford helps run the Bold Start Training Stables at Breach Lane, Wootton Bassett. Business partner Brian Woodfield, 46, confirmed Mr Witheford had received several calls from protestors, but he denied the circus allegations.

"Mombassa, the last zebra we trained, ended up in a circus," he said. "But this one definitely will not. When we give Masai back to its owner it will go to a park in Devon."

Most of the complaints the stables received were from people arguing animals should not be displayed purely for human enjoyment.

"That is because the programme was misleading," said Mr Woodfield. "We are not putting the animal on display."

He stressed no whips were involved in the training.

"There is no cruelty involved at all," he said. "The reason Masai reared is because a cameraman got too close and upset him."

Mr Witheford is well known in Wiltshire racing and equestrian circles for his ground-breaking training techniques.

He uses a combination of body language and eye contact to train animals to accept a saddle rather than the traditional "breaking in" method.

After training Mombassa in June the stables wanted to prove their success was not a one-off fluke. Now after a week of training, Mr Witheford says he is delighted with the 18-month-old Masai's progress.

"His forward nature indicated he would be a fast learner," he said. "I can't believe how well he has responded."

An RSPCA spokesman said: "Mr Witheford's methods are not cruel on the face of it. But wild animals should be allowed to do what they do naturally."

He confirmed the society would not condone the zebra being used as part of a circus act. "The RSPCA is opposed to making wild animals do tricks," he said.

Gary Witheford

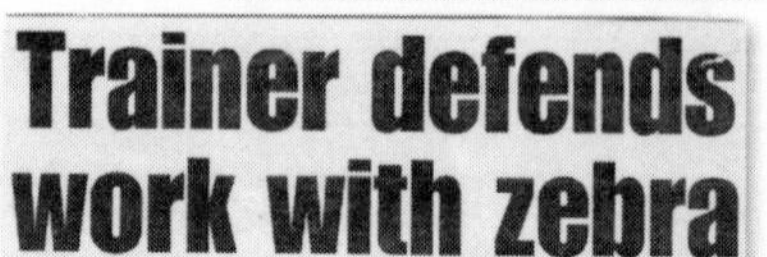

Trainer defends work with zebra

No circus for Masai, he says

By DAVID PEARCE

"The TV programme was misleading" ... horse trainer ... zebra ridden by Nikki Davis

A WOOTTON Bassett horse trainer is at the centre of a row over his pioneering efforts to train zebras.

Gary Witheford, 36, has received a string of calls from concerned animal lovers after he was shown on television training one of the animals.

In the programme the zebra reared up and fell over but was uninjured.

It was suggested that the animal would end up performing in a circus and showed an interview with an outraged animal rights campaigner.

Mr Witheford helps run the Bold Start Training Stables, Breach Lane, Wootton Bassett.

Business partner Brian Woodfield, 46, denied the circus allegations.

"Mombassa, the last zebra we trained, ended up in a circus," he said. "But this one definitely will not.

"When we give Masai back to its owner it will go to a park in Devon."

Most of the complaints the stables received were from people arguing animals should not be displayed purely for human enjoyment.

"That is because the programme was misleading," said Mr Woodfield. "We are not putting this animal on display."

He stressed no whips were involved in the training process.

"There is no cruelty involved at all," he said. "The reason Masai reared is because a camera man got too close and upset him."

Mr Witheford is well known in Wiltshire racing and equestrian ci[rcles for] his ground-breaki[ng train]ing techniques.

He uses a combi[nation of] body language and [eye con]tact to train anima[ls to ac]cept a saddle rather [than the] traditional "break[ing in"] method.

After training M[ombassa] in June the stables [wanted] to prove their succ[ess was] not a one-off fluke.

After a week of t[raining] Mr Witheford is d[elighted] with the 18-mo[nth-old] Masai's progress."

Trainer stunned by animal lovers' protests after 'misleading' TV item

'Cruelty' row over zebras

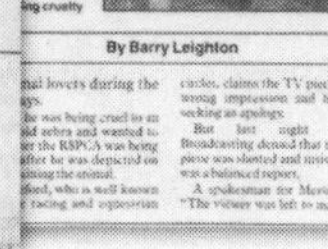

By Barry Leighton

Horse and Rider

TV spotlight shines on trainer's skills

THERE is never a dull moment at the Old Dairy training yard, at Westcourt, near Burbage. It's home to a variety of equines including Masai the zebra and Cleo, a tiny Shetland foal.

In addition there's a goat who thinks she's a bulldozer, an Alsatian who loves annoying the zebra, and a hairy cockerel called Tina Turner.

This week is particularly exciting because the BBC started filming at the Old Dairy on Monday.

Specialist horse-trainer Gary Withe[ford] ...

... called Here and Now, to be shown at 7.30pm on November 17.

A lot of new horses arrived last weekend, including Snoopy, a nappy, nappy New Forest pony; Molly, who won't load, and Holly a 15-year-old mare who, bucks, rears and runs backwards.

On Monday Jeffrey arrived, a handsome black nine-year-old Hanoverian gelding, who was competing in International Level dressage and has started rearing, spinning round and bolting.

Anger over TV report

Trainer in zebra row

■ Training in progress . . . Gary Witheford of Wootton Bassett with Masai the zebra

A HORSE trainer is at the centre of a row over his pioneering efforts to train zebras.

Gary Witheford, 36, received a string of calls from animal lovers after he was shown on TV training one of the animals.

The zebra reared up and fell over but was uninjured.

The programme suggested it would end up performing in a circus.

Mr Witheford helps run the Bold Start Training Stables, Breach Lane, Wootton Bassett.

Business partner Brian Woodfield, 46, denied the circus allegations.

"Mombasa, the last zebra we trained, ended up in a circus," he said.

"But this one definitely will not.

"When we give Masai back to its owner it will go to a park in Devon."

"The programme was misleading," said Mr Woodfield. "We are not putting this animal on display."

He stressed no whips were involved in the training process.

"There is no cruelty involved at all. The reason Masai reared is because a camera man got too close and upset him."

Mr Witheford is well known in Wiltshire racing and equestrian circles for his ground-breaking training techniques.

He uses a combination of body language and eye contact to train animals to accept a saddle rather than the traditional "breaking in" method.

After training Mombasa in June the stables wanted to prove their success was not a fluke.

This time their approach was quite different. In the pen there was a rake we used for levelling the sand: the zebra shied at it, reared up and fell over. He was fine, but the TV film focused on it. The line had changed from, 'This guy is fantastic to be breaking a zebra and this girl to ride it,' to, 'Why are they interfering with a wild animal?' Before I knew it the animal rights people were on to me. I had one guy on the phone saying that the Grand National should be banned, no horse should be ridden and cows shouldn't be shot: serious shouting and screaming for half an hour. He said he was going to kill us – 'You people should not be allowed in this world.' For a while it was quite scary.

Mind you, it taught me a big lesson in how quickly the press and everyone can turn. Don't forget, six months before I had been thinking I was the dog's bollocks: going off to this new yard, leaving poor Sue Bond in the lurch, and now I was realising, God help us, that these things can destroy you. I was quite humbled. You meet the same people coming down as you do going up, and it's much harder coming down. You have got to remember that. Yes, it taught me a big lesson.

The new place might have been bigger and had a floodlit arena and everything, but I had issues with the owner. By April I had to get away, and came to the place where I am now. It was almost derelict – just four stables and a barn and some land, and a couple of happy hackers in a cottage. I found a new couple to give me the backing. I would have a car, a monthly wage and a share in the business. At the time it seemed a good deal. Little did I know.

Meanwhile, the previous owner tried to stop us taking the horses away. He managed to hold on to Masai. He wasn't his to keep, as he had been given to me by the Chipperfields, so I had to get them involved, and in the end Mary's husband Roger Cawley brought him over to me.

But during the drive Masai tried to jump out, and got his front legs hung up on the back of the trailer. He had severed both tendons, and when we lowered the ramp there was blood everywhere. The poor thing could hardly stand up. So I rang the vet, Jenny Hall, who came over and looked at him: the tendon sheath had gone, and she said, 'You are probably better putting him down.'

Jenny had never worked on a zebra or anything like it before, and was wondering what drugs to give it; meanwhile I've got Mary Chipperfield on the phone saying, 'These zebras are much tougher than you think. I've seen them with half a bloody shoulder missing where a lion's got hold of it, and they come through that.' Jenny managed to get an anaesthetic into Masai and operated on him on a sheet out in the front yard. She flushed everything she could out of the tendon sheath and started stitching up. She must have been there two or three hours, as after she had stitched one leg we had to turn the zebra over to do the other one. She had the guy who would become her husband with her. They had only just started going out – don't know what he must have made of it all. It was madness.

But the Chipperfields were right. Next morning Masai could hobble about a bit, and Jenny said, 'Well, that's the first 12 hours over with: never thought we would even get to that.' By the end of the week he was putting all his weight on his forelegs – he was almost normal. After that he was really just a mascot, and although the horses were quite shocked when they first saw a zebra they got used to them, and in the summer they all liked to stand with them because there were never any flies on a zebra. It's the smell they give off, and the texture of the skin. Never any flies – amazing.

We did get Masai started with Nicky a couple of times, but he had never really taken to it the way Mombassa had. What was worse is that after throwing her off he would kneel down and try and bite her. I would have to pull him off her. He did it a couple of times before his accident, but afterwards he was worse. He was probably hurting anyway, so we stopped with him. He and Nicky never really got on, and she could not lead him. When she and another girl tried to lead him out from his box to the paddocks he just took off like a bullock, with the two of them hanging on to the ropes and being pulled along as if they were water-skiing.

But he was only tiny, Masai. He was so small that we cut 'zebra flaps' in the fences between paddocks, so he could just wander wherever he wanted. He and I had a real bond, and he would come in and lie next to me, like he had done that first day that Meridian had never showed on TV. He didn't lie down like a horse does, but stretched right out with his head on my lap. He had a sort of donkey bray – they call it a bark – and you could call him. On 5 November, the first year here at Westcourt, we had ripped all the hedges down and old rails and things, and made a massive bonfire, put potatoes on the fire in silver foil and had a few drinks. It was the foggiest of nights but I said, 'There is a zebra out there: I will call him, and he will come in.' So I called out to Masai a couple of times, and there we all were sitting around this massive bonfire with flames going 20 foot into the air – and this little zebra comes in. He stood right by the fire. I said, 'I've got him.' It was a real magic moment, being able to call up what was still a wild animal, and for it to come in and stand next to us by the fire.

Masai died a couple of years later. He had reacted badly after we tried worming him: Jenny Hall tried to give him a blood transfusion but he just pegged out. As I said, he was not as good as Mombassa, but he did show that you could get just about any flight animal started if you did the Pressure/Release, Call-Up thing with them in a pen. We did it with a llama once. It was called Naughty Nelson: we got a saddle on it at the Cotswold Show and Nicky rode it, but it turned its neck right round and spat in her face!

There was one more zebra that came, and he taught me a very different lesson. He was much bigger, nearly 14.2. Compared to Masai he was a huge bull of a thing. He came from a zoo at Marwell; he'd had a tooth abscess, so they had taken him

Mombassa II in the field with Arnie. Barrister is to their left.

away to operate and drain it, but when they put him back with the other zebras he started to kill his young – it must have been a dominance thing. For some reason we called him Mombassa like the first one – better say Mombassa II. They asked me if I would take him, and I thought it would be a good idea, as the zebra had become a bit of a calling-card for us. I didn't ever really trust him, but he settled in, and people would be amazed to see a zebra in the field. It's not something you expect in the middle of the English countryside.

Mombassa would find his own friends. He got on very well with a horse called Barrister – they would play and dance together in the field. It would be good to watch, until one day, even though they were only playing, Barrister kicked him too hard and broke his shoulder, and we had to put Mombassa down. But his big day had come a bit earlier than this, and what he did was quite extraordinary.

We had been sent this big grey thoroughbred colt with quite a nice name – something to do with 'Eagles' – but we always called him TK. He was a stunning horse, and the owner thought he was going to win everything, but he was an absolute pig: you couldn't lead him. He was a thug, a real thug, and randy too: he would jump on anything, shouting and screaming. I had worked its mother for the owner: the mare had been a box-walker and would never settle in the field – just gallop up and down the fence. I had calmed her down, so now I'd been sent TK. He was more difficult.

One morning he broke out of the round pen – just took it on and broke it down. One of the girls was working him, and perhaps she had put a bit too much pressure on him, but he's the only horse that has ever done it. Anyway, TK is now loose in the field, and goes hollering up to the first horse he sees, which is Jazz. Big mistake, because Jazz is a 17.2 black and white stallion, a bit like a shire horse. TK thinks he is a big shot, but Jazz is a giant, and just shoos him away. TK gallops on, crashes straight through a set of rails, and ends up in the bottom paddock, which has a couple of horses, some sheep – and Mombassa. TK starts hollering and pushing the others around, but Mombassa isn't having it. As TK comes dancing up, Mombassa rushes in, seizes him by the throat and pins him to the ground.

I had been at Lingfield and was just coming in when all this was happening. There was this big bully screaming like a scalded cat – what a baby! I ran down and pulled Mombassa off, but he kept running round and trying to grab TK again. Eventually I got TK back into the stable. He had blood all over his neck, so we had to clean him up and keep him in. But, do you know what? Next day he was a different horse. Completely different horse, to the point where instead of having to put a chifney on him just to lead him from the box to the round pen, now you could put a head collar on and walk over with no bother. He could still be a bit nippy with a farrier, but we used to give him a broom handle to chew on. Otherwise he was absolutely fine. He went off to be an eventer – William Fox-Pitt even came to have a look at him.

Looking back, the lesson all that taught me is that if a horse, for whatever reason, has become a complete thug, and is making everything impossible for everyone, you can change him almost immediately if you humiliate him. You don't have to handle it violently like Mombassa did. You can tie up their legs so they have to roll down on the ground. They are flight animals, and now you have deprived them of their flight. I didn't realise it then, but later came to know that when they are on the ground you can actually walk over their body. Yes, walk right on them. If you pull a horse's near fore up tight, and pull its head in towards you, it will slowly lean in and lie down. No hitting, nothing violent. That's when you walk over their body. They just accept it. I call it 'Putting them on the floor,' and when they get up they are different. You have taken their legs away: you've taken the flight out of them.

The horse is sensitive and quite intelligent, but it is still a simple animal, and to a horse that's become a danger to itself and others this is a simple lesson: it says, stop throwing your weight around, because there's always someone bigger or stronger than you. It may even be a zebra.

'Jazz was a big boy – a huge piebald, gypsy cob.'

10 | Getting the Points

Stefan Forsman is a fairly extraordinary man, and an even more extraordinary horseman – direct-staring, shaven-headed: an animal lover with a touch of steel about him. When Gary first met Stefan in the summer of 1997, 'it was as if a light bulb had switched on.'

Two years younger than Gary, Forsman had a horse and country background in his native Sweden, and had been to America to work with horses and cattle on the Flying E Ranch in Montana. But he had also trained in martial arts and boxing, as well as doing slightly mysterious combat work in war zones with the Swedish Army. His current operation offers courses in Wilderness Survival under the rubric, 'Get Lost in the Wild', in Self-Defence with the challenging slogan that 'Peace is not the absence of conflict: it is the mastery of conflict.' But above all, Stefan offers 'Forsmanship'.

In 1997, Forsman held a three-day clinic at the Woolstone Stud near the village of Uffington, below its famous White Horse on the Berkshire Downs. The 20 or so people who had signed up were blown away by the directness of the Forsman method: this was Monty Roberts with the gloves off. For whereas the great Californian's 'Join-Up' technique stresses that man and horse should seek a 50-50 partnership, Forsman demands submission: that man should be the leader. There is no brutality in the lunging and turning disciplines that he puts the horses through in a round pen similar to that used by Roberts, but there is an insistence that they turn at four specific points on the ring: North, South, East and West. 'The Points' are at the heart of Forsmanship.

The theory is that when the horse has submitted to these central instructions, it has accepted the man as its leader. That done, the animal will, within reason, accept whatever other instructions it might be given. So at Uffington on that last weekend of May a formerly neurotic half-bred called Brandy became amenable enough to walk into a trailer on its own, a flighty quarter horse called Sumo accepted being completely covered in plastic as if it was nothing more than a change of rug, and a randy stallion called Beau Saab walked calmly under a canvas awning and then past his mares with almost monk-like decorum.

All the time, Stefan stressed the need for leadership. Today he says that with innate leadership you can make his method work without any previous knowledge of horses. But back in 1997, he was about taking Natural Horsemanship to a new level. He was all about challenge. That suited Gary, because challenge was exactly what he was getting from a horse called All That Jazz.

Jazz was a big boy – so big that we have a picture of him with three of us on his back. He was a massive great black and white stallion, a huge, piebald gypsy cob, and he was the guy who was later to shoo away the randy TK before it was mauled by Mombassa. Jazz had been sent over from Shrewton by John and Jackie Young: she had been a good race rider, had bought him to cross with thoroughbred mares in the hope of making the perfect sports horse, and wanted me to get him started.

He would challenge you: yes, doing The Points in our round pen, Jazz would challenge me right to the button. Where most horses will get used to turning when you want them, Jazz would come to within two foot of me before he would turn. It was as if he was playing a game of dare, to see which of us was going to move first. Of course stallions will take you on: that is their natural instinct – a horse is all about 'flight or fight', and if a stallion is to be king of the herd he has to fight. So he is going to challenge, but you must face him down.

I knew this and had been doing it within my version of the Monty Roberts method: it was all about making horses turn, about Pressure and Release. But there was this thing about a 50-50 partnership which all seemed a bit too negative to me: I felt we should be more positive. So when I went to see Stefan

Stefan Forsman. His 'Forsmanship' hit home with me – real leadership.

Forsman and he talked about needing to be the leader, that light came on – for when I dealt with horses, I had to be the leader.

He had heard about me because of the zebras, and came over to Westcourt after the clinics to have a look. Then he invited me over to Norway, and I went there for a week to watch him work. Yes, he was much more positive – almost aggressive really. But he made sense of where I had been going in my head. When I came back from Norway I put The Points at the centre of what I did. All horses that came to me had to do The Points. It's such a central part of my version of Natural Horsemanship that I want to give you an outline of what we do in the round pen – and I think every rider with a horse, every child with a pony, should have an understanding of this. This is something I've worked on for years and I'm wary of people trying this at home in case they misread their horse.

Basically, putting a horse through The Points is how I set out to control its movement, to get inside its head, to have at the end what we call Call-Up, when the horse will actually walk across to me and is prepared to follow me around the ring. It can look like magic, but it's not: it's what the Indians in Americas have been doing for years.

But before we do anything we need the horse to understand the very basics of Pressure and Release, and we do that just on the halter. Stefan had a normal rope halter – I think it was an Australian one – but I think the kind I have now, the Double Diamond brand used by Buck Brannaman, the Montana 'Horse Whisperer', is better. It's a nylon rope halter with knotted pressure points on the top of the head, under the chin and under the throat: while you don't pull at a horse, if it backs off and pulls at you, the knots tighten. But as the knots are half-hitches, if the horse stops pulling back, it eases off – hence our words Pressure and Release. Some people have tried to make these halters out of sailing rope, but they tangle up. I like these ones because they are idiot-proof.

So the first thing you do is put the halter on, and establish your leadership. That may sound big, but it just means that you face the horse and check it back on the halter, and bring it forward when you want. The best place to do this is actually in the box. You look him direct in the eye, with your shoulders up, and drive him back, and then relax your shoulders and ease your posture as you ask him forward. You will know when the horse gets this, because he will drop his head and lick and chew with his lips and teeth: it is his language of acceptance.

When he has done that – which I promise you he will – you go into the round pen and, before anything else, get him to walk behind you. Most horses are taught to lead with their head in front of the owner, which means they have no clear leader, and can easily start barging you around. So, once in the round pen you stand up square, look him in the eye, and send him back like you did before. Then turn around and walk away in front of him with your body passive and relaxed, and a full metre and a half of rein for him to follow behind.

If he tries to push up either side, you gently stop, and send him back again, and put him in behind you. That metre and a half is his comfort zone, because to a horse the most important things are his legs: they are his instruments of flight, and if he gets too close, he makes his legs vulnerable. Watch horses walking up to the water trough in the field, and they don't line up together: one is the leader – in the herd it is usually an old mare – and the others are prepared to accept it. Your horse, my horse, must accept me as a leader, and so I will walk him round the pen, and then I will 'park' him. Yes, this is when the memory of watching those Westerns in Singapore kicks in: the cowboys hiding behind a boulder, guns blazing, and their horses just stood there!

What you do in the ring is to turn and face the horse, which will make him stop and stand in front of you. Then you tie a knot at the end of the lead rope, and drop it to the ground: the horse will feel it heavy, and dip his head to avoid carrying the load. You step back, but he will not follow you. If he does, you take him back to where he was, and 'park' him again. He will accept it: his leader has told him.

Now to The Points. What we are really doing here is using a horse's sense of flight to drive him round the ring into situations where 'doors' close and open for him – it's as though you're pushing him through a sort of mental maze out of which he is happy to be led. At the end he will want to come to you.

We say there are four equidistant 'points' around the ring: A, B, C, D – call them what you like, provided you stick to it. What we do is control the horse's movements so as to make him turn at the point you want him to. You do this by forceful and passive body language, by the kissing sound, and by the flourish and occasional use of the whip, but only when necessary, and even then only a sharp flick around the fetlocks.

For example, let's use point C as the turning-point. You start by loose schooling the horse in the ring with only his halter on. Stand in the centre of the ring, as big and positive as possible, and make a loud kissing noise. This applies pressure to the horse, and he will naturally want to flight, which in this case means cantering round the edge of the ring. Once you have forced him into action and got the speed you want, relax your body language, release the pressure, and let him continue while you pivot on the spot with the line of your body behind his shoulder. You want him to be watching you, and you can see he is doing this if his inside ear is bent in your direction.

You let him continue this until he dips his head and licks and chews. That's him talking to you, telling you he is accepting you and is prepared for his next instruction. So as he next passes point A you go all positive, run in behind him making the kissing sound and put your back to the wall – then go passive. He will naturally go to the opposite end of the pen, point C, because it's the furthest point away from you. He doesn't want to go on in that direction because it will take him closer to this man who has just driven him away. The door at C is closed.

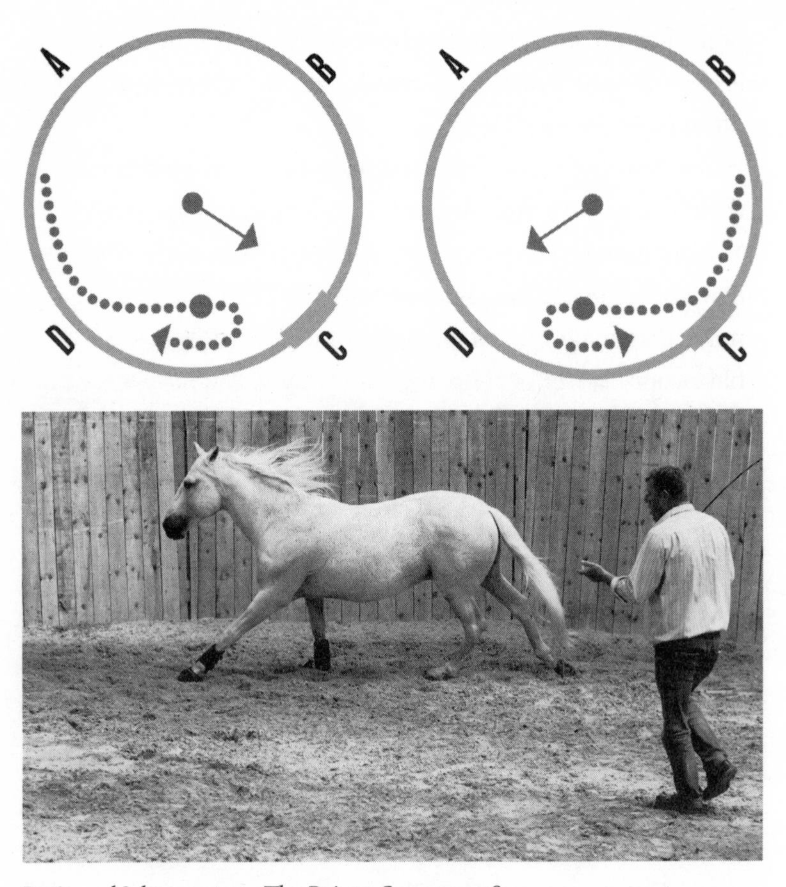

Brujo and I demonstrate The Points. See page 238.

Once there, he will turn and look at you, and begin to double back. As he does this you come back towards the centre, but looking relaxed and passive, which means you are opening the door at A for him to continue through. And because you are relaxed and passive, he is reassured that he has done well. You encourage him on for a couple of circuits, but then when he gets to point A next time you repeat the earlier process. As before, he will stop at point C, because it is the furthest and safest point both from you and in his head, because the 'door' ahead is closed. As before, he will turn in and, as before, you send him off in the other direction.

You have now controlled the horse's movements coming *off* the fence in both directions. The next step is more challenging. You are going to turn him at point C again, but this time it will be *into* the fence. You set him off as before, but this time you move diagonally across his path as he approaches point C. You have your best 'positive' body look on, and you have the whip in your outside hand. You are closing the door in his face at point C.

If the horse does not turn, he is taking you on and trying to gain leadership. So now you will have to step in towards him and crack the whip. If it continues towards you, you will need to give him a sharp smack around the shins. Whatever happens, do not back off, as backing off is a sign to the horse that he can control your movements, and next time he will try to push you harder. As I said at the beginning of this chapter, a horse like Jazz would challenge me right to the button. Yet on the line, he would turn like the others. Most horses will do it without too much bother.

But the important thing about this 'door-slamming' turn is that because you have challenged the horse he will turn defensively away from you, which in his terms means swinging his hind quarters, his main weapons, towards you. He will turn *into* the fence.

Once you have got him circling the ring in the other direction, you repeat the operation to make the opposite turn. Once again you wait until he is approaching point C, only now you have the whip in the other hand, and your angle of movement is counter to your previous one. This turn may be even more of a challenge for him, and if he goes slightly past your demanded point C it is essential you repeat the exercise to make sure he knows that he has to turn when you want him to: that he has to do what his leader tells him.

If you are working a horse for the first time, completing one 'Point' is enough for the first session. But when you have done all four Points cleanly – that is, when you have got him to turn both *away from* and *into* the fence on each of the four corners of the ring – you can move into Call-Up. What happens here is that you run to one of the Points – let's say that first point A – and he will normally reach point C opposite you, and turn and wait for your next instruction. You then move to a position 45 degrees from his eye-line, so he has to turn his head to see you. When he looks at you, stay still, because with his neck at this unusual angle his first move will be forward to release the pressure in his neck. At this stage you must smoothly back up, drawing the horse towards you until you are up against the fence.

He will come up to you. Rub him between the eyes to tell him he is a good lad but no patting, I don't believe in that. Then walk away along the fence line, and he will follow you. If he doesn't, or if he breaks away, go positive again and make him work a couple of circuits before repeating the process. I do not normally get to this Call-Up stage until about three or four days into a horse's programme, but when it's done it means that you and he have a full understanding of each other. It's really quite straightforward to do and, as you will see, all sorts of people have done it under instruction. But it does make a difference. Every rider, every kid who wants to understand their horse, should do it. What's more, if they can't do it, then that horse or pony is too much for them. If you can't manage the horse from the ground, you won't do it very well from the saddle. Parents put kids on ponies they can't manage, and then blame the pony. They should face up to The Points first.

Of course, it's hard to describe it on paper. The best way to do it is to take someone into the ring and guide them through the process on foot. They walk round the outside of the ring as the horse does, and discover their natural inclination to run when I confront them with a raised whip as I do the horses. What's more, they will want to get as far away as possible which, in a 60-foot ring, means you will naturally run to the opposite Point to where you were threatened, and turn and face where the threat came from.

But the key thing is that I chose where you have to turn. I would be calling the shots, and you would be accepting it. I am putting on the pressure and you would be happy when I ease off and give you release. It may sound strange, but when you walk people through it they really do understand. And they are not even 'animals of flight' like horses are.

Anyway, this all began to work for me. I was doing a lot of what I had been doing before, but it had more structure now. And of course The Points was always only the start of what we needed to do. A lot of horses that came to us then – well, it is often the same now – were sent because they had got very flighty and aggressive: because they had got too much for their owners: because they had become the leader.

One of these at the time of Jazz was a white Connemara stallion called Silver Rogue. He would take me on in the ring, but I could get him to accept the turns needed in the Points, and after he had done that we put him through the plastic routine that Stefan Forsman had done at that Uffington clinic. Ever since learning about Baltic Love and the clippers, I believed you needed to push apparently scary things on to horses when they reacted, rather than backing away and making them feel that panic was the right reaction. Horses don't like plastic – they're very wary of it – and they don't like the crackly noise it makes, so the way Stefan had wrapped that flighty horse all over in plastic made sense to me. It certainly helped with Silver Rogue.

But the real problem with him was that he would kick the **** out of his box. You would hear him going *bang, bang, bang*. He would destroy the place. In the end I put a set of hobbles on him – it was as simple as that: just locked one leg to the other with a pair of hobbles. He couldn't kick: I had disabled him: he had to accept me as the leader. He gave up kicking there and then.

Westcourt was still pretty basic – just a few boxes in this old dairy barn and a sand ring where we could put the round pen. But we were being sent all sorts of horses. There was a New Forest pony called Snoopy who had gone all nappy, a mare called Holly who had started rearing and running backwards, and a black Hanoverian thing called Jeffrey who had got into the habit of spinning around and bolting. We put them through The Points, and we sorted them out. People were pleased. Jacqui Broadridge contacted the BBC, who came down to do a half-hour documentary for the *Here and Now* show. In many ways it put us on the map.

If you look carefully at the footage you will see a figure in the background raking all the stones to make it look nice. It's Cozy Powell! He was back from a tour and about to go off on another one with Brian May. It was funny, really, because there is this rock star roaring up on his Harley Davidson and walking in just as if he was my brother or something, and saying, 'Come on, get the coffee on.' Very few people actually knew him like that because he didn't have that many friends. I never asked him for tickets or an autograph or anything, because to me he was just another person, another person with problems: he used to come out and do the painting with me. At Westcourt he said, 'I can't do the horses, but I'll cut the lawns and get it all tidy.' He loved that. He had a sit-on mower, and if anyone drove on his grass, God help them. He laid that bit of tarmac in the middle of the yard. I still miss him a lot.

But the greatest thing about Cozy was that he loved what I did, and he pushed me on. I was very shy and didn't believe in myself – like thinking I couldn't speak at a demonstration. At one of the very first ones we did at Wadswick I even switched the microphone off because I felt so embarrassed. I could not do it: I said to Cozy, 'I have got to have a script to get through this.' 'No,' he told me, 'you can't do a script, you've just got to come over as yourself and it will become natural.' Fair do's to

Cozy Powell – a rock star on horse back!

Cozy, it has. He used to say, 'You'll hold the crowd – you've just got to believe in what you do.' It took me a long time. I used to be so scared of those demos and then – I can't remember what horse it was – I thought, 'Well, I am ****ing good: I do believe in what I do.'

But the rest of my life was not going well. I had finally moved out earlier in 1997. Maybe Julie and I had been through too much, what with the house being repossessed and my obsession with the horses. I had tried to make it work but I couldn't. Half the time I had been staying at Wootton Bassett anyway. At Westcourt I slept in a corner of the Portakabin office, sometimes even in the car. Craig wanted to come with me – sometimes he slept in the car too.

If that didn't make sense, neither did the business side of things. But what had seemed like a good idea with the second owners had turned into a nightmare. My friend Cozy would come to the rescue.

But first he had another tour with Brian May. He did not come back until March, and when he did he had a problem. He was sore from a motorbike accident, but something else was depressing him much more. He had a girl he could not get out of his head – couldn't stop talking about her. I had known him for about 15 years, and there had been quite a lot of '****ing this and shagging that', but this was different. Of course, she was married to someone, but Cozy just could not get her out of his mind.

It was 5 April, the fourth anniversary of my father's death, and that morning we were painting in the yard. I was down and Cozy was very down. I think he was quite a manic-depressive, anyway – a lot of these stars are, aren't they? Suddenly he said, 'I can't handle this.' I said, 'Don't be so bloody stupid.' But the next thing is that he's left: he gets a call from her and sets off down the M4. He had a big black Saab 9000. He had got near Bristol when she rang again, and he was talking to her when she heard him say, 'Oh, shit,' and the line cut out. He had been doing 104 mph and was thrown out of the window. He died before they could get him to hospital. The box he was painting that morning is still unfinished, and it will stay that way until I move or die.

Brian May and Jools Holland came to the funeral, and I scattered Cozy's ashes at Bold Start Farm where I had first met him. The day before he died we'd had a letter agreeing to the Key Man insurance he had taken out for me, but a few days later another letter arrived saying that while it had been agreed, it had not actually been implemented, so would have to be void. Cozy had been a Barnardo's Boy and so didn't seem to have any family, but late in the day it looked like some relatives emerged and inherited the lot, right down to the sit-on mowers Cozy had brought down here to cut the grass for me.

It was a strange, strange time, because only a fortnight after Cozy died, my new girlfriend Pauline had a bad fall. She suffered a terrible head injury and was in a coma for a long time. I was going up and down to Bristol to see her, but she would never recognize me. My marriage was over, my children weren't with me, my best friend had died, and now this. A nice couple called Sarah and Will Long had come to live in the village: I remember talking to Sarah and just collapsing on the grass crying and crying.

If I'd had my gun then I would definitely have used it.

'It was like being exposed to a different language.'

11 | Arnie and Flight

Sarah and Will Long are two of the sanest people in this whole story. Sarah has worked at a senior level in IT at a string of major companies; Will, after 12 years as a Royal Navy helicopter pilot, is still involved in aviation and remains a qualified helicopter pilot. Their coming to Westcourt in 1996 proved a saving grace: for in 1998, Gary was in melt-down. They like him very much, but they're realistic: 'He is fantastic with horses,' says Will, 'but crap with people and money.'

They had met him one evening in the Three Horse Shoes in Burbage. Sarah was complaining that the ex-racehorse she had just given away had proved an expensive failure. Gary said he would find her another, and a deal was done whereby he found it, trained it and used it all week, and she then had something decent to enjoy at the weekends. Will hadn't ridden much since a bad experience with a horse of his sister's, but he had a farming background, and was happy to help with painting and mucking-out while his wife was in the saddle.

In the epitome of neighbourliness, Sarah and Will became partners in Gary's business which, like the Old Dairy itself, they found 'in a parlous state'. They faced down the previous owners, closed Cozy and Gary's company, and sifted through the debts. Sarah, with her business experience, accompanied Gary to see some of his principal creditors: she didn't promise them much, but she pledged that debts would eventually be repaid. That all of them have now been honoured is because she was realistic about Gary's flaws as well as an admirer of his gifts. People still remember 'the look' she would give when Witheford was getting above himself. 'You can't control Gary,' she says with easy authority, 'so the best thing is to let him do his thing, and then work around him to give a structure that can protect both him and the business.'

When Will left the Navy he got involved, converted one of the stables into an office, took Gary to talk at Rotary Clubs and Women's Institutes, and strengthened links with the racing industry. By the time the Longs stepped aside and subsequently moved to Hertfordshire, a sensible business model had been established.

The three of them remain friends, although Will speaks wryly of the 'adrenalin addiction' that Gary gets from dealing with difficult horses, and of his need 'to move from one drama to another, and if there isn't another he creates it'. But he also speaks of life-enhancing moments: of how Gary put him in the round pen 'with a colt full of testosterone, and told me what to do. I must have been sweating fear, but when I stopped, it stopped; when I turned left, it turned left. Two days later I was standing in the yard as the riders were gathering: without any prompting, this colt walked over and nudged me. It was like being exposed to a different language.'

It's a language that can save horses – even if in some cases they are too scared to listen.

Arnie is the most nervous horse – the most frightened horse I've ever worked with. In many ways he has been the most influential horse in my whole life, even more than Brujo. I have learned so much from him: of how dangerous horses can be when they are really frightened: how they can strike out with their forelegs – they want to kill you. With Arnie it was sheer terror: fight and flight.

He was a three-year-old colt when I first had him, a bay Lusitano this guy in Middle Wallop had shipped up with a load of horses from Portugal. I got a phone call that they had this horse, but they couldn't catch it – couldn't touch it. They said, 'You had better come over and try something, or we will have to shoot it.' When I got there, it was in the box, and it was terrified. It had white scars on its legs where the hobbles had been, and a mark on its shoulder where it had been hot-branded. Its only contact with humans would have been pain-related. At Middle Wallop all they could do was offer a carrot, and he would eat it and run away. When I went into the box with him all he wanted to do was back off, and strike out at me with his forelegs.

I told them I couldn't handle him at their place, but needed to get him over to my yard where it would be quiet and relaxed. So I managed to slip a lunge line over him like a lasso, got him tied really tight to the side, slid on a head collar and attached a lead rope to it. We drove the lorry in as close to the stable as we could, but when we opened the door he just went crazy, absolutely crazy. He got loose, and the rope ripped and blistered my hands. We had no control at all.

So he galloped off into the Wallops: I was after him, but he had these long lunge lines whipping round his legs, and the more they flapped the more he ran. We finally managed to trap him by a tree, and then got the lorry into the road next to him, and just herded him up the ramp. Westcourt wasn't like it is now: it only had four stables then, so when we got back we reversed the lorry as close as we could, and then ran this terrified colt down the ramp and straight into his box, and left him.

Then I began to work with him, and that's when I learned a lot about what you can do with horses at night. It's quieter, and they're quieter in themselves, than during the day with people all around. I would start at 10 or 11 o'clock at night; there would be no one else about, and I would begin by chucking the lunge line at him. He'd kick at it and run up the wall. OK: I had to be tactful, but I knew I had to put the pressure on him so he would be pleased when I took the pressure off. He began to understand. I got to a point where I could throw the lunge line over him, much like I did with that zebra. I threw it over so it would drop to the floor on the other side of him, and then I got a stick and dragged the lunge line towards me, threaded it through the buckle, and then tightened it so I had a line around his neck.

This is where he taught me about touch. Once I'd got him, I didn't pull him: I let him come to me. It would be quiet, and I would stand with my back to him and wait, and then I would feel that first touch on my shoulder. He would come up and I could feel him breathe on me. That taught me, 'OK, you've touched me; now I'm going to touch you.' To begin with I was only able to touch him on the nose; then I could touch him on the neck; work down the neck, and then get him on the shoulder. But he was never safe. If you grabbed at him he would leap away and then strike out at you with his front legs. I had to be very, very careful, as I didn't have as many people around as I do now: I didn't have Craig – I was on my own except for Nicky, who was three-foot-nothing. It was all trial and error. Nicky used to say, 'How did you do that?' 'Why did you do that?' 'How did you know to do that?' I would say, 'I don't know – I don't know what it was.' It was just the instinct to do the next thing that would help him through.

If I could get him to accept me, I was thinking, I'd then be able to stand in the centre of the box and get a pad and a saddle on him. That's what you can do with most horses, but he would keep turning and facing you, ready to strike out. So that's when I started 'sacking him'. I would throw sacks over his back, and then pull them down his neck and around his legs. I would get him to walk over some plastic sheeting, and then wrap him up in it just as we had done with Stefan Forsman. It was a question of hard work and plenty of it, before we even thought of putting a rider on him, but we got to a stage where he would do The Points, and we got a saddle and bridle on him.

Then the owner came round and said, 'I think we can deal with him now. I've got this Portuguese guy coming over, and he can break him for me,' and took him back to his farm, this massive place near Middle Wallop. But Arnie was still a colt back then, and was always going to be too much for them. A couple of months later the owner rang up and said, 'I don't need this shit. You have him or I'll shoot him – just take the horse for what he is, and if you sell him, give me some money.'

Arnie had gone back to wildness. He was snarling and having a go – he had all that fight in him. I had got him to the stage where I could get a head collar on him, but when I went to do it at Middle Wallop he just went berserk, absolutely berserk: he got loose and burst out of the stables, broke through a set of post-and-rails, and bolted up the lane. We managed to catch him before he got on to the main road, but he was a real bugger to put on the lorry, a real swine.

When I got him home the first thing I did was to get Jenny Hall to come and cut him, but it didn't change his behaviour much: even now he's a very aggressive horse, and back then if we turned him out he would be very hard to catch. One day the only way we could do it was for a vet to come over and 'dart' him – shoot a sedative into him. Nowadays you can catch him in the stable all right, but if you turn him out in the paddock you can't: what you have to do is to open the gate, call him up, and he follows you into the barn. Let someone shut the doors behind you, and he walks into his stable – it's as if the work I'd done with him in the evenings and nights had held: his stable was a safe place – it was his bedroom.

That's why nowadays I never muck out horses when they're in the stable. From dealing with Arnie I came to think that they need their bedroom, their space on their own. Arnie felt safe in his own stable, so he began to accept us. We could take him for walks, loads and loads of walks – John, an old guy who still helps in the yard, had never been very horsey, but he would take Arnie off all over the place.

I felt he was just lost: a lost soul, if you like. He felt so trapped – he was more flighty than those zebras. People kept saying, 'He's costing you a lot of money' – but he was teaching me so much! It was being such a nervous horse that made him so good in demonstrations: he was happier in the pen working than he would be outside – you've got all those people on the outside of the pen to scare the living daylights out of him, so he looks for the somebody he knows, and when I'm in there on my own he feels safe. Because he's such a flighty animal he actually learnt to work The Points very quickly: he worked out for himself that he had to turn around, twist around and go away from me as I shut and opened the 'doors' in front of him. He became really switched on to how I wanted him.

Nicky riding Arnie at Peterborough Show – I was in tears.

Working Arnie under plastic – he has taught me so much.

Finally, over three days at the Peterborough Show, I actually started him, got Nicky on him, and had him ridden away. At the end of it I couldn't speak: I was in tears that this horse with all those scars on his legs, that had been beaten and become so terrified, would accept me enough to do this. I was so choked up that I got on him myself and rode him out of the ring – the hairs come up on my neck now even thinking of it. And yet if someone tried to get on him now, Arnie would bury them.

He is the ultimate example of what a horse will do if he puts his trust in you. He still gets scared now, at 19 years of age – if you press him he would run clean through a set of post-and-rails – but if I do The Points with him in the pen and get him to stand still, he lets me crack the lunge whip near his ears without a flinch. He's with me, and it's my whip, so there's nothing to fear. Yes, he's a very strange horse, but he's taught me so much.

The other horse I took to the Peterborough Show was very different. He was just about the most intelligent horse I have ever had. He's turned completely white now, but back then he was a very pretty, coloured, dipped-back Andalusian-type horse Mary Chipperfield had paid 50 quid for when she found him as a foal tied to the back of a gypsy caravan. He was about 15.2, quite flashy, with a long mane, and she thought he would make a circus horse. He was called Tulsa.

He was three when I got him. Mary had not got Tulsa to the circus yet, but she had been working him in the ring. He would

Tulsa would follow me everywhere – even into the office.

canter round, and when she shouted, '*Allez!*' he would stop and spin round one way and then the other like a pirouette, and then canter off in the opposite direction. I carried on with that voice work, and I used to do a lot of play with him – he would do The Points and then take a bow at the end of them. Teaching a horse to bow or lie down is really quite easy: what you do is pull a horse's near foreleg up tight and backwards towards its tail: to keep his balance the horse will lean back, stretching his off fore out in front of him, and dropping his nose right to the ground. If you push him a little he will dip further and lie down. Foals often do it the first time the farrier picks up their feet.

Tulsa got so good at it that he would stretch back and bow just by my tapping him above the knee on the near fore. He would do so much for me just by voice-command: I could put a straw bale in the centre of the ring and he would put his forelegs up and then pirouette around it. Mary would reward him with nuts or Polos, but I don't agree with that: I think you can reassure without sweets. I rewarded Tulsa just by stroking; he knew when he had done well. If I do want to reward with food, I put it on the floor – giving something in the hand, especially if it is Joe Public, is just inviting a horse to bite. It's one of my pet hates, for it's very easy to feed little foals and home-bred horses with sweets and bits of carrots, but when they get bigger, especially if they are colts who are often very 'toothy', they start ripping your pockets out looking for their reward.

I always reward Arnie with a stroke, and what's more, I never pat horses: I stroke or scratch them. One of the things I always say in my demos is, 'Never pat your horse.' Because they're flight animals, patting desensitises them in just the way you don't want: their skin is so sensitive they'll shake a fly off when it lands. While they may panic over clippers or plastic and it's therefore a good thing to put Pressure and Release on them to get them desensitised and used to the worry, it is just the opposite with the rewarding touch. You *want* the horse to be sensitive to your feel. If you just put your finger on his neck and rub, he will like it. But if you pat him every time you see him, it will be like the man who keeps coming up and slapping you on the back: quite soon you cross the road to avoid him. Yes, scratch or stroke, but never pat your horse.

We had Tulsa for three or four years, but then a couple whose pony had a kissing spine and become a runaway came over, and their daughters fell in love with him. They were so keen to have Tulsa that I sold him to them one Saturday for £4,000 in readies, which was big money for me back then, and would buy a lot of buckets and more hay and feed. Trouble was, on the Thursday I had given Tulsa to Craig as his horse. The new owners were absolutely delighted with him, and still send me Christmas cards with his picture; Craig has never forgiven me!

Tulsa could make people go 'Wow', but at Peterborough he also gave them a big laugh. For he would do everything without even a halter on. After Call-Up he would walk behind me, and one of the things we would do is to get four people to hold up each corner of a big sheet of plastic and drop it on me and the horse. At the Peterborough demo I was wired up with a radio mike and asked for a volunteer from the audience. Out came this woman with high heels and fluorescent green mini-skirt.

We walked under the plastic canopy, and when they dropped it I said to her, as a bit of banter, 'Is your boyfriend here?' She didn't realise the mike was on and thought I was chatting her up: 'Yes,' she said, 'but I can get rid of him.' 'Help,' I said – 'get me out of here!' The audience thought it was hilarious. Not so sure about the boyfriend.

This kind of banter helped take me out of myself, and I began to use it to settle people. I still use it to relax people, especially riders going into the starting stalls: it takes their mind off what they are doing. It works with women who are getting worried – but back then they all began thinking I fancied them. Then they started wanting it, and I ended up shagging half of them – because although I was free, I didn't want a relationship. So to me it was just, 'Oh, OK, if we go out, I will give you one tonight, and then I will go back to the bird I had the day before.' I think it's harder for a woman than it is for a man: a bloke can just do it and walk away, but a woman wants all that lovey, touchy stuff and everything that goes with it.

The thing is, I was this 38-year-old guy, broken away from his wife, setting up a business, and I had more Joe Public horses than racehorses then: a lot of fluffy horses with their owners, married women, or separated women, or women unhappy in their marriages – and don't forget, you've got husbands that go and play golf on a Saturday and Sunday, or watch football, and their wives are out there riding the horses that their husbands can't sort out for them. All of a sudden there's this guy who can sort their horse out, and it's all, 'Oh, you're my hero!' Quite a few of them hoped I would sort them out too, but afterwards there would be a lot of husbands out there after me. I had one guy come round with a shotgun one day and threaten to '****ing blow my head off'. I became a frigging shagaholic. Looking back, it was an absolute disaster, and I was a lot to blame.

'I was lucky to have Craig . . .'

12 | On the Floor

Craig Witheford is a quieter and more laid-back character than his father, which in view of the circumstances is no bad thing. That he has come through so many traumas to become Gary's most trusted rider and assistant must be one of the great feats of filial forbearance – especially as at 16 he had given up horses and signed up for a carpentry course in Chippenham.

However, the reasons for Craig's change of mind show that it's not only in equine chemistry that he is his father's son. 'There were a couple of work-experience girls in the yard,' he says, 'and there was this kid called Leo riding a yearling that was pulling all sorts of shapes. Of course, these two girls fancied him, and I didn't like that, so I said to Dad, "I'm going to ride that tomorrow." I sat on it, rode it, and it bucked and broncoed, and I never looked back. I cancelled the carpentry course. I said, "No, I want to work for my dad."'

Today he talks with both sang-froid and poignancy of the personal and professional journeys he has had to make. His riding enthusiasm had seemed permanently doused when a first pony smashed him in the face, and was hardly rekindled by being grabbed and thrown over a rail by Boomer, the Morgan stallion turned savage by what proved to be a brain haemorrhage. Even when Craig returned to the saddle – he did have four flat races but didn't get a buzz from the game – he has had to pay his dues: he tells of the time a filly (subsequently diagnosed with severe stomach ulcers) suddenly stopped and hurled herself over backwards on top of him.

Craig will never have the freakish, angst-induced gifts of his father, but his own interpretation of the family method is even easier to understand, and hardly less effective. To watch him talking of a morning to someone as forcefully intelligent as champion trainer John Gosden is to see a young expert expounding an opinion in his own right. 'Horse whispering' or other such tags are often misleading; what Craig Witheford delivers on behalf of his father is simply horsemanship in the most fundamental sense. Maybe Natural Horsemanship is not so bad a term after all.

Craig also speaks with some humour about the family difficulties he has had to handle – of how he was locked in his bedroom by one of Gary's later girlfriends who was jealous of the time he spent with his father in the stables, and of how in the unhappiness of his parents' break-up Gary could not bear to come to the house, and so the son would walk half a mile to the top of Hungerford Hill to be collected by him. 'I'm a sucker for feeling sorry for people,' he says calmly. 'I felt sorry that Dad was on his own, and I wanted to make sure I was with him. Plus, my mum is not an animal lover, nor are my sisters, but I always was. So I saw it as the only way I was going to spend time with Dad, and be around horses and other animals. I was determined to keep the contact, and if I hadn't done, I would not be doing what I am now.'

One morning I got a phone call. It was a Newmarket number, and I thought, 'Ooh, who's this?' It was Luca Cumani, a major trainer who has won two Derbys. 'I've got this horse Newnham,' says Luca. 'We can get it in the stalls by itself, but as soon as you put another horse in it just goes crazy and starts attacking it.' I was on my own in the office, so I did the normal bullshit of turning the pages near the telephone and saying, 'I'm a bit busy at the moment, but I think we might be able to get you in, perhaps tomorrow?'

Next day Luca Cumani's lorry pulls in here and drops the ramp. I've got the stalls close to the house, so I take the horse and say to Cumani's lads, 'While you're here, we'll just put it in, and you can see that we got started.' It walks straight across and into the stalls: in, out; in, out: no problem. They said they'd taken half an hour to get it on the lorry to leave Newmarket, so I also walked it in and out of the lorry. 'I think we'll be fine,' I said, 'but I will give the boss a call after tomorrow and tell him what I think.'

So next day it comes out, and I put it in the stalls with another horse next to it, and **** me, it's straight over the top and it's grabbed this other horse by the neck and is trying to bite it, attack it any way. It's roaring like a stallion at the other horse, which is ****ing screaming with fear. We had to open the stall and let it go. I rang Luca and said, 'This isn't going to work: I think you're going to have to cut it.' 'OK,' he says, 'but it's home bred in Ireland – can you phone the owners and tell them what he's like?' So I called them up, and there was a story there. At home the horse had become a bully. Originally it had been very, very weak, it was getting bullied, and they'd even wondered about sending it into training at all. But then it became one of those horses who suddenly start to grow and get strong, and think, 'Right: now I will have you bastards back.'

We had him cut, and you could ride him around all right, but as soon as you put something into the stalls beside him he would try and climb over to attack it. Even with a blindfold he could smell them and hear them, and go crazy. I thought he might not do it with a filly, so I put one of them in, but he did it just the same. I was at a loss to know what to do – but this is where I really learned about putting horses on the floor. I didn't just pull his near fore up to make him lie down: I put a set of hobbles on him in front, tied one back leg to them, pulled the other one forward, and he just flopped down.

I got an old Shetland pony and I just walked it around and around him. He was angry. He fought and he screamed, but he was all trussed up so he couldn't do anything – he couldn't harm himself, or me. I left him there until he finally gave up, then I untied him and walked him straight into the stalls with the hobbles on, but not tied together. Then I put another horse alongside – a filly: I wanted to test him. He just stood there: he absolutely stood there. He didn't move. I brought him out, brought the other horse out. Then I put him in and brought a horse in each side of him, and still he never moved. I thought, 'Gotcha! I've gotcha!'

I phoned Luca Cumani and told him the horse could come back, but don't bother with the stalls until he is ready to run, and I will come up a week before to put him in and make sure he is OK. A month or so later I get a phone call, and drive over to Newmarket with Craig, who was very new to it all then. It's the first time I've worked for Luca Cumani, and everybody is looking at us: here's Gary Witheford with this little lad. It was eyes everywhere – it felt really uncomfortable.

Luca Cumani comes over and says, 'You won't get him in the stalls – we've been trying the last few days.' I could see Craig was about to say, 'You told him, Dad – you told him not to do it!' But you can't say that to Luca Cumani, so I said, 'Leave it, Craig,' took a set of hobbles out of the boot and walked back into Newnham's box. 'What are you doing?' they said. 'Putting a set of hobbles on' – and they went, '*Really?*'

So I put the hobbles on him, pushed him from the side so he wobbled, took them off, legged Craig up on him, put one of my halters on, and walked him straight into the stalls. Everybody was like, little heads everywhere. Then they brought the lead horse out, and said, 'No horse ever beats this lead horse out.' So I go, 'OK', walk him and Craig into the stalls, and, one, two, three, *bang, whoosh*, and he's ****ing beat the lead horse out. Luca and the others stood with their mouths open, I promise you. So I say, 'Have you got another horse? This time put it and the lead horse in first, and we will put him in between them.' They bring out the other one and, one, two, three, *bang, whoosh*, he beats both of them out again.

The following Monday he was running at Windsor. When he was brought in to the box to be saddled I put the hobbles on and pushed him sideways, just as I did back in Newmarket. He cantered down to the start, walked in the stalls, stood there like a lamb, absolutely perfect, and he ran and finished second. He was placed five times for them, then he was sold and later won four in a row on the all-weather. 'Putting him on the floor' had solved his problem, but the frustrating thing is that some people still don't want to understand. I had a guy ring me up and say he had a horse who needed to be put on the floor because 'he wants a ****ing good hiding'. It breaks my heart that people think I change horse's minds by giving them a beating.

One day at Newbury I was standing talking to some trainers outside the weighing-room and another came up and said, 'I have a couple of horses for you, Gary. They want some "Withefording" – a good ****ing beating because they are ****ing taking the piss.' Two of the trainers walked off and one of those left, Brian Meehan, said, 'That was right out of order.' I was really upset, and when I got home I sent an email saying I was not prepared to be spoken to like that, and I was not prepared to do business with anyone who thought I was into giving horses a beating. We have since made it up, but at the time it really hurt – that anyone could think I want to hurt horses, when my ideas are all about understanding them better and consequently making life easier for them.

If you saw me working you would realise that I only use 'putting on the floor' when a horse is in danger of making itself unmanageable – when, if things were to get much worse, it would be a danger to everyone else, and have to be shot. But it was from Arnie that I also learned that when they are on the floor, you can rub the lesson in by sitting or walking on them, and it is a fact that, once you have walked on a difficult horse, it can be much easier to ride. Newnham is the only horse I have ever had to do twice, and if they won't improve after that you probably need to get rid of them.

I learned to use it with really stroppy yearlings, older stalls horses, or big eventer types who would not let you on their backs. I started to think, 'OK: if you won't let me on, let me put you on the floor and walk all over you, which you will like a lot less than me sitting on your back.' At one stage Arnie used to throw himself on the floor – he had such an element of flight about him that if you asked him to come back he would turn and just flip over on the floor and lie still – it was a form of sulking. So I would actually sit on him – I would say, 'All right: if you want to throw yourself on the floor, I will just sit on top of you.' Horses get like knots in their brains, and we have to try and untangle them.

But it's not a risk-free business, and I had a dreadful experience with a filly of Godolphin's in Dubai. Two days before I saw her she had reared up and cracked her head in the saddling boxes at Meydan. As I was over there on a trip they asked me to put her through some stalls to make sure she had got over the experience. But when I asked her to go near the stalls all she wanted to do was rear. I didn't trust her to go through a stalls test, and decided to put her on the floor. So I strapped up her leg and she leant back – and then literally flopped her head down and bled to death on the ground. Because it was Godolphin they took the trouble to have a full post-mortem, and discovered that she had fractured her skull banging her head in the box in that incident a couple of days earlier, and when she had lain down one of the fractures had gone into her brain. Brian Powell, the assistant trainer who had asked me over, took me out for a drink, but a lot of people spread the story that I had killed something. I remember ringing home in tears. It still makes me feel sick to think about it.

I never want to hurt anything. I don't want to get hurt, and I don't take chances in this game, because all too often I am dealing with the worst of cases, and I have got to know their body language. A horse was sent to us one day: we led it up to the stalls, it just smelt them as they do, took a step back, *whoosh*, straight over backwards. I turned round and said, 'Is this horse insured? Because it's going to kill itself.' 'Yeah, yeah,' they said. The second time, I led it up myself, so it would be no one else's responsibility. The horse looked at the stalls and, *whoosh*, straight over backwards again – I'm not talking just rearing up and slipping, but all four legs off the ground and right over onto its back. It lay there as if it was dead, then suddenly shook itself and got up. But it did walk strangely, so I thought it might be concussed, and got the vet out. He looked at it and thought it might have detached its retinas. So the next day they got another vet who studies eyes to have a look.

The other vet came over the next day, looked at its eyes and said it was fine. I said to the trainer, 'Look, this horse has built up such a fear factor that I don't think it will ever go into the stalls. It might do anything.' He said, 'No, it has to win a flat race.' I told the vet I wanted him around while I worked this horse. I led it out to the front of the stalls and, *whoosh*, straight over backwards. It hit its head on the ground, blood came out of its eyes, out of its nose – stone dead. I rang up the owner and said, 'Is the horse insured?' 'No,' he said: 'we must see to that.'

So what makes me think of things like that? Because with all the experience I've now had, I do see things with horses, three or four seconds before anybody else. I'll say, this is going to swing to the left; this one's going to swing to the right, before it even does it. People say, 'How do you know that?' I don't know, but I watch their eyes, their body language and simple things like the muscle across their chest. When that tightens just that little bit it means they are about to move towards you, and so you should release any pressure you have on them. It's as subtle and as simple as that – because if you pull them, they will pull against you.

Of course, I had already been dealing with odd horses, and putting them in the stalls, for a long time. One of the first was also one of the very worst. Another Batchworth was a filly of Eric Wheeler's when I was at Wootton Bassett. I went down to Eric's place at Pangbourne and she reared, turned round in the stalls and jumped out of the back gates. You would never believe it – and she didn't just do it once: she did it about four times. She would also lie down, literally lie down, and go passive. But we did get her into the stalls, and Eric used to take me with him when she was racing. When she won at Redcar the commentator said, 'Another Batchworth is in front, and the rest are just chasing shadows.'

She and Eric's other filly Batchworth Belle took me all over the country. In 1998 Batchworth Belle won at Epsom, and next year she won at Newmarket, and was placed three times at Ascot. To start with, the stalls handlers treated me like ****, but I was beginning to get a reputation. Rodney Ellis from the hunt kennels told Richard Hannon I could sort out one of his horses in the stalls. I said I would take him, without admitting that I did not have any stalls of my own, and had to build a sort of imitation out of railway sleepers.

Me and my boy.

The Batchworths were home bred and a problem with a lot of these horses is that they come from places that have old staff. It's OK having the knowledge, but if you get a dodgy horse you need the brave people to get in with them, and when you get older you tend to stay away from the dodgy ones because you can't be bothered any more. So when I go into these yards, often my job is not just to look after the horses: it's to look after the riders, the people around me.

I was lucky to have Craig. He is so fantastic, because at the age of seven or eight he was determined he was going to live with his dad. Very few sons would go with dads – they're normally mummy's boys. Craig did and does love his mum, but he said, 'Oh, no, I'm going with you.' I can remember him picking up his Thomas the Tank Engine duvet, and I didn't even have anywhere to live.

He stayed at school in Hungerford, so I used to run him there in the mornings, and Nicky or John used to pick him up if I was racing. Every day when he'd come back the poor little bugger used to walk into this yard to see if the building work had gone forward at all. He was determined with horses, too, and has plenty of bottle. He is really good in the stalls, even though he has had a few knocks. I remember early on at one of our demos, someone produced an unbroken horse, and we started it, and Craig rode it away in front of his mother and sisters, who were all in tears. He and I are very different, and we have our moments, as all fathers and sons do, and one year he even walked out at Christmas for a while. But he gets as upset as I do when we get criticised, and I just try and say, 'Let the horses do the talking.' You'd be amazed at how many people actually come up and say, 'Thank you for showing us it can be different.'

'He became a friend and he became a mate, a soul mate if you like.'

13 | Brujo

Suzanne Witheford was Suzanne Vesey-Thompson back then. She had a five-year-old daughter, a six-month-old son, and a horse who would not walk up the ramp into the horse box. The Gary who came to load it had already had a very bad day.

To be exact, he had got up at four in the morning to drive what was then a very rickety old lorry down to Kent. There he had to collect a stroppy, hardly-handled, coloured stallion from a field twenty minutes' battling walk from the nearest place to park the wagon. It was the hottest day of the year, and when he finally got back to Burbage with blistered hands and black with sweat the news from Sarah Long was not welcome. Some woman near Newbury was meant to bring her horse over, but she couldn't load it.

'He obviously sussed my horse out as soon as he looked at it,' remembers Suze. 'It was a big, spoiled thing that I had only had for three weeks. Gary put the halter on, did a bit of his checking-back thing and said, "This is a very angry horse." He introduced it to the lorry ramp and then said, "This is going to throw itself down on the floor." That's exactly what happened: it threw itself down on the ramp like a child having a tantrum in a supermarket. Gary said, "In a minute he'll get up and he'll walk in." It was almost as if the horse understood the words. It got up, licked and chewed, and walked into the lorry. Then Gary unloaded and loaded it three or four times and said, "Right: we'll go now."'

Unlike the rest of Gary's conquests, conversation was not immediately followed by an attempt at carnal relations. Over the next couple of years Suze became a friend and a Sunday helper as she rode her horse under his supervision, did chores around the stables, and began to volunteer in other areas. She may have disappointed her father by not joining the family dental business in Marlow, but she had made a success of a career in events marketing, and she and her then-husband were running a design business in Newbury.

'I had no idea it would lead to this,' she says diplomatically. 'But I could see what a great horseman he was, and it reminded me of the events business where some very, very talented carpenters could not take their business forward. Sarah Long had managed to impose some structure, and Alice was manning the phone, doing the book-keeping and running the diary. But I could see such potential. I thought I could help.'

Be careful what you wish for. Suzanne and Gary were married in Bath on 11 December 2008. It has not been easy, but the potential has been delivered, and more. Even if horses, and especially one white Andalusian stallion, were always likely always to come first . . .

The demo was on the lawn right in front of Highclere Castle. It was part of the Highclere Festival of the Horse, and its setting is now known to everyone who watches TV as *Downton Abbey*. It was on the bank holiday weekend at the close of August 2002, and featured eventers, show-jumpers, dressage-to-music, some ladies jumping side-saddle, a dog show, and us. It was the biggest test yet for Brujo. And, since it was Craig's first major demo and his mother and sisters were there to watch, it was the biggest test for me.

Highclere Castle is Downton Abbey to most people. But the demo there in 2002 was one of my most important days.

Brujo had come a long way in the three months since I had first seen him chained to a wall in Andalucia in the spring of 2002. The trek all the way from Girona must have been an ordeal – it would have been the first trip he had ever done, all the way from Spain and on to the ferry. When he finally arrived, the top of his tail was absolutely raw where he had sat down in the box. Even now you have to be quite careful how you load him, because of the bad memories he must have.

But from that first day in Spain, he was special: the horse I had always wanted. It's a strange old feeling, but it had almost been like seeing a puppy dog: you could have 20 puppies in a box, but you pick one out because his eyes say, 'Look at me.' I don't know what it was: I just said, 'I want him. I need him as much as he needs me.'

I didn't pay for him: I just paid 250 quid for transport. Between me and you and the gatepost, I'm pretty sure Brian Oak-

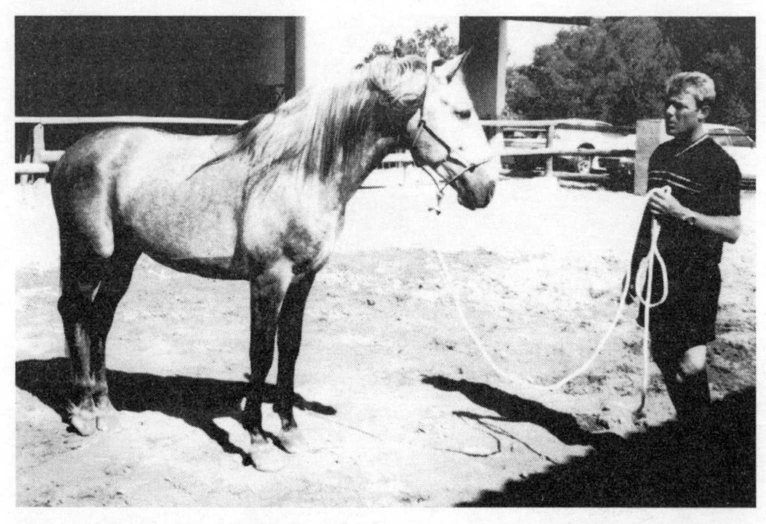

Meeting Brujo that first day in Girona in 2002. Minutes before he had been the saddest horse I had ever seen.

Brujo on form at the Malton Open Day 2012 and enjoying his roll afterwards.

Clockwise from top left:
Arnie at Lingfield.
Arnie at Kempton.
Brujo and Craig at Lingfield.
Arnie at the Cotswold Show.

Relaxing in Cuba.

Above: Brujo at Kempton. *Right:* Nika on a 'starter' at Kempton. Minutes later he was as good as gold. *Centre right:* 'Called up'. *Bottom:* 'Starting' a colt by Brujo at the Cotswold Show. *Below:* Arnie standing calm while I crack the whip near his ears at Lingfield.

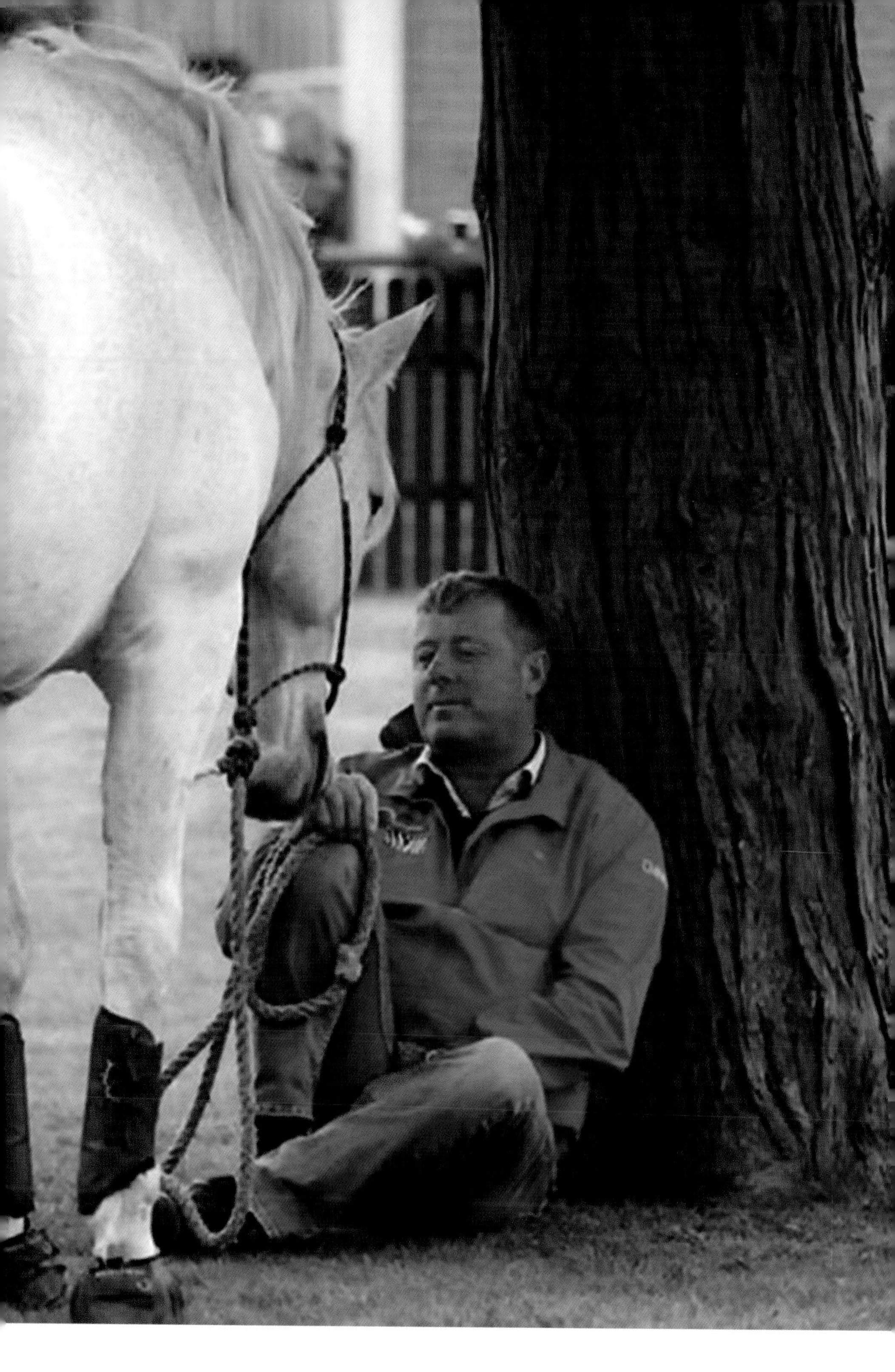

Brujo and I take a break during a demo.

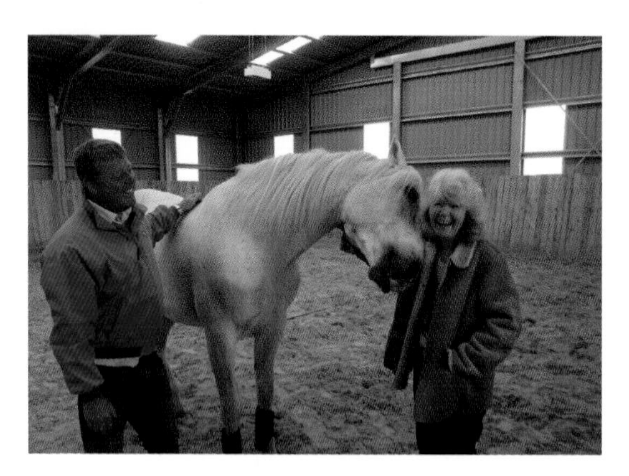

Clockwise form top left: Jilly Cooper comes to visit; Brough Scott and me at Cheltenham 2014
was teaching him to write; Craig and me going to work at Royal Ascot 2014 – we had four wi
ners; with the staff at The Palm Restaurant, near Marlborough – our wonderful local.

Below: Playing at Westcourt.

Top: Arnie at home – what a hero.

Above left: With Suze.

Above right: My other love – or is it the other way round?

Above: Suze and me with the dogs at Westcourt.

Below: At home.

ley's wife Susie paid meat money for him behind the scenes. Brian runs Oakley Coachbuilders, and that April he and Susie had arranged to meet me in Girona: I was physically exhausted with all that was happening in my life, and the Oakleys had said, 'You need a break away from working flat-out – let's take you away for a long weekend.' I ended up working horses and bringing another horse back, so talk about a 'busman's holiday.'

On Brujo's first day here I just put a head collar on, so as to have a little play with him, and he just felt really good. His box is where my workshop is now, and it was right next to where I had my mobile home. I had a door cut out to make an extra window, and so he was literally standing above me. At nights he loved to watch the TV: as soon as you turned it off he would just kick that door until you turned it back on again. So I had to sleep with the TV on.

I started taking him out in the evenings for long, long walks on my halter, like you do with a puppy. I wanted to get his confidence back, because he'd obviously had such a bad experience in Spain. They said he was bad, and he must have learned a trick or two about bucking and dropping his shoulder and getting you off. You never know the truth, but there were those marks on his nose where they had put chains on him, to try and keep his head up. They had ripped his nose open – when I first saw him he had an open flesh wound with maggots and flies on it. There must have been a reason why he did what he did.

He walked behind me, always behind me – wouldn't walk alongside. I didn't have to turn and check him at all. That's what proved to me that horses do not want to be led by the side. He taught me about having a lead rope of a decent length, at least a metre and a half, for the horse needs to walk that distance behind you. If a horse doesn't want to lead, why should he. How can he look at you as a leader if his head is in front of you? Brujo loved being behind me: he was saying, 'OK: you're my leader.'

In the evenings we would walk for miles – out around the village, up the hills, everywhere. Then one day I stopped, put the lead rope round his neck, got on, and rode him home bareback. He was grand: he never bucked, and he's never bucked since he left Spain. He became a friend and a mate – a soul mate, if you like: somebody I could relate to. He can be a worrier: sometimes you can see him frown – but he smiles as well. When you put someone like Craig on bareback, you can actually see him smiling – we have pictures up on the wall where he's got a cheeky little grin on his face. He's a stallion, but he really worried the first time we brought a mare for him, and he didn't know what to do. You can take him out with the head collar and he will stand all day eating grass – and he'll come up when we have a barbecue. He loves a glass of red wine.

He's been central to the development of my demos, because he has such a presence. He's almost 17 hands, much bigger than most Andalusians, and he is the most intelligent horse I have ever come across. In the ring he will challenge me, read me and respond to little more than a look: he really tries for me. But he will also do his turn, with all this prancing and stallion behaviour the crowd love to watch. Then, once it's over, he just goes, 'OK, you've got me,' and he'll stand in the middle of a show ring with kids pulling his tail, walking underneath, tweaking his ears, and he'll never kick out or anything. And to think that this was once a terrified colt chained up to a wall on the way to the knacker's yard. He's amazing, Brujo.

Brujo at his best.

But he was still only a three-year-old when we took him to Highclere that August Bank Holiday and started him off then and there. We took him through the Points and Call-Up, put the saddle on him, and finally Katie Edwards, who was working for us then, rode him away. It was a wonderful turn, and Lady Carnarvon absolutely fell in love with him. She had a grey Arab mare called Azure which she later bred to Brujo, but when the foal was born the mare rejected it and the foal was sent over to us. As a foster mother we tried a mare called A Little Hot that belonged to Sarah and Will Long. It was quite a performance because when the foal arrived you would never have seen such a tiny, miserable little thing. But A Little Hot took to him and made a really good mother. Her own foal seemed to know what was expected of him. For when we took him away, he saw his mates in the next field, trotted up to the five-bar gate, jumped over clean as a whistle, and never looked back.

But for me Brujo was only one part of the Highclere demonstration. We were also given an unbroken yearling, and Craig and I started her off as we do all of ours. She did everything right, and then I laid Craig across her and he finally got a leg either side and we rode her around. There, in front of their eyes, a completely unbroken filly had been bridled and backed and ridden away by a 16-year-old kid. It was something most of those watching thought took a full month or more, and here it had happened in less than half an hour. In its own way it was very moving for everyone, and for our family in particular, for Julie had brought Gemma and Callie over, and Craig had done it right there in front of them. They were all in tears. 'Yeah,' says Craig – 'they always cry.' But in truth, it was very special for all of us – and especially for me.

Demos had become very important, and Sue Walker was a huge help in fixing them up for us. She and her husband Steve were both school teachers, and they were very good to me: I often used to drop in and have dinner with them on the way back from visiting Pauline in hospital. Sue would have booked the Highclere demo, and earlier in 2002 she got us to Equus, the big horse show at the Excel up on the river in London's Docklands. This was a big challenge, because I had never been to an arena anything like this before: there were 15,000 people for the shows. It was a lot of pressure on me and on the horses. We had Arnie, a grey Portuguese Lusitano stallion called Lustrosso, and a nervous little pony called Humphrey. For Arnie and Lustrosso the pressure was probably a bonus, because it made them sharper: they would move quickly away round the ring when I ran at them, check and turn when I made them, and were actually pleased to walk after me when I wanted them to come to Call-Up.

They were spectacular horses, anyway. The Andalusians are used in the bullring, so they have to turn and think even if some of the poor sods just end up as the picador's horse being gored through that heavy padding. The Lusitanos are very much the same – they and the Andalusians were considered the same breed until about 1960. We got Lustrosso from Margaret Chipperfield because he had turned savage. We managed to change him, and later sold him to a man in Ireland who used to let him come into the house – we still get Christmas cards.

Lustrosso was great because, like Arnie and Brujo, he would challenge you, and when you drove him away and then called him up it looked terrific – you could even get him to take a bow. But the horse who was a real success at Equus was Humphrey. He was a grey, only about 13 hands, and had come to us as a remedial pony from a South African lady called Shelley who said he was taking fright at everything, and we wanted to show we could calm him by doing the work we do with plastic. When he came into the ring he was so nervous his legs trembled, all wobbly like in a cartoon. I made him do the Points and Call-Up, then follow me over the plastic that we'd laid out on the floor of the arena, then have it wrapped all over him, and finally walk under a canopy held by four spectators. The way the little fellow changed and accepted everything we did to him really brought the house down.

There was another reason for me to be nervous before that show. Suze and I were beginning to link up, but before the Equus show I had gone off on holiday to Mexico with an old girlfriend without telling her. When Suze found out, she was pretty unhappy, and as I'd come direct from the airport she didn't see me until I arrived at the show – she and Craig had brought the horses down from Wiltshire. It was all very awkward, but in fact, the Mexico trip had its benefits, because I realised there was no future in rekindling that old relationship, and Suze and I began to get closer and closer. Her marriage was ending, and we finally started living together in 2003. She has had to put up with a lot, but she is the best thing that has happened to me. Maybe even more than Brujo!

One of the worst things we had to deal with were some horrible 'slasher attacks' in 2005 on four of Brujo's foals. The first was in June to a chestnut filly we called Rioja: I went out in the morning and found this little thing hobbling around with blood all over its hind legs – somebody had slashed a deep cut under its tail. It had obviously been done by someone who knew a bit about horses and had a helper who could hold the filly while they slashed her. I thought it must have been someone with a grudge against me, and that seemed even more likely when they did another filly in the same way. But the police were sure it was odder than that: there had been these things before, apparently – a whole spate of them in Hampshire in 1993 and 1994, and 12 in three villages in Derbyshire and South Yorkshire in 2003. It had been some sort of cult: they targeted the sexual organs and even drank the blood.

Horse whisperer believes attack on horse is linked to two others

Police appeal for help after colt left slashed

By Nigel Kerton
nkerton@newswilts.co.uk

HORSE whisperer Gary Witheford has revealed that an attack on a horse currently being investigated by police was the third since June.

Last week four-month-old colt Mio was left with a foot long slash from its anus to its genitals at Mr Witheford's Westcourt Stables in Burbage.

Police are investigating the incident and say they want to hear from anyone who saw suspicious activity in the vicinity of the stables.

Mr Witheford said Mio was the third horse to receive similar horrific slash wounds. Two fillies, also four months old, received almost identical cuts, one in June and another in July, he revealed.

Police were called to stables in South Marston, near Swindon, in August where a horse received a neck wound and to Calne in July where a filly received an injury to her sexual organs.

A police source said the view was taken that the injury to the horse at South Marston could have been accidental.

Police decided not to investigate how the horse at Calne had been wounded after a vet said his inspection of the injuries had been inconclusive.

There is an underlying fear in the equestrian world that there could be a replay of the 1993-94 period when an attacker dubbed the horse ripper struck on numerous occasions at stables in Wiltshire.

They were part of a series of frenzied attacks that left horses injured across a number of West counties.

However, research on the internet this week revealed reports of similar attacks on horses as far away as Scotland where investigations linked the horse wounding with the occult.

Through their Horsewatch co-ordinators, Wiltshire police have been advising all horse owners to make regular checks on their animals.

Mr Witheford, who has gained a national reputation for dealing with problem horses, is convinced that Mio and the other two horses did not injure themselves accidentally and were the victims of a sick attacker. He said Mio was in a paddock at the time and he had no idea what sort of person could inflict such injuries, which had to be stitched by the stables' vet.

Mr Witheford said: "The wound is horrific. A straight, deep slash.

"Mio can just about walk but he is in a lot of discomfort."

The young colt was traumatised said the trainer, and would need to regain his confidence with humans.

Vets who examined the two fillies wounded in the summer said they could not have been caused acciden

COMFORTING CUDDLE: Gary Witheford tends to Mio but he fears it will take time for the c

Horse slasher leaves stables in fear

Up and down the country animals have been stabbed and mutilated but the culprits are elusive, reports Ben Macintyre

'The animals never forget. There is a very sick person out there'

In September they came back and did a three-month-old colt of Brujo's called Mio: they split him from his anus right through to his genitals. It was a foot-long slash and he was very sick: it was terribly slow to heal, as he kept bursting the stitches when he moved, poor little thing. There had been reports of a man in a flat cap and a white van, but they never caught anyone. Then in November whoever it was came back and slashed Rioja again, cutting her deep across the stomach; the wound got infected and she nearly died. The story became national news: *The Times* had a big article by Ben Macintyre with a map showing other attacks in Kent, Suffolk, Carlisle and the New Forest. It still felt like someone was targeting me, but the police were sure it was this cult thing, even if they never found anyone.

'The authorities are much more reasonable nowadays but sometimes they still find it very hard to listen.'

14 | Stress in Stalls

John Gosden's background is the polar opposite to Gary Witheford's. The tall, athletic and intelligent son of the brilliant trainer Towser Gosden, he left Cambridge with a degree in Economics and athletics Blues at both the discus and the javelin, and initially spurned the idea of following in his father's footsteps to go and work in property in Venezuela.

But at the stage when Gary was abandoning racing for better returns at Marley Tiles, John returned to it, as assistant first to Sir Noel Murless in Newmarket, and then to the even more legendary Vincent O'Brien in Tipperary, before starting on his own in 1979 in California. From there an unbroken victory march stretches over 2,500 races, from Breeders' Cup triumphs in Hollywood Park to his present Derby-winning, Champion Trainer renown at the very top of the British tree.

As important as Gosden's eminence has been his informed, untroubled eloquence when internal squabbles look set to tear apart the jealous, feuding structures of the British racing game. One such issue arose in the spring of 2005, when the authorities decided to replace the life-expired starting stalls at British racecourses with a new Australian design. What followed on the first of May was an ugly fracture to a handler's leg at Newmarket when a two-year-old colt called Envision panicked before the start.

It emerged that, despite the apparent success of some trials with older horses on the all-weather at Wolverhampton over the winter, these Australian Steriline starting stalls had lower bars at the back and unpadded protruding boards against the side, causing horses to kick and the contraptions to shake and rattle, setting off chain reactions amongst other runners. John Gosden spoke out firmly: 'Something must be done to avoid more accidents,' he said. 'The pointless bars on the tailgates should be removed, the running boards should be fully padded as in America, and the framework drilled and filled with foam to absorb the tinny sound.'

Some heed was taken, but not enough. In July, the trainer Mick Channon wrote an impassioned letter to the Racing Post *that began: 'Does someone have to be killed before the authorities take any notice?' and Gosden followed up with a scathing and detailed broadside which concluded, 'This situation can no longer be conveniently ignored. Health and safety and animal welfare are issues we need to take seriously, rather than playing Russian roulette at the beginning of every race.'*

All parties were duly summoned to a showdown discussion at the British Horseracing Authority in London, modifications were agreed and understanding gradually resumed. However, the furore had been a wake-up call for the industry. 'I have seen a jockey killed in a stalls accident in the States,' said John Gosden. 'They are the most dangerous part of flat racing.'

Gosden has not got where he has without being able to draw on experts. Throughout this saga it was to Gary Witheford that he turned for an opinion, and in the 2014 season it was still Witheford he had supervising the stalls entry of his Classic star Kingman. 'It's very reassuring, especially for jockeys, when Gary is down at the start,' he says. 'Gary has a profound understanding of the horse and its psyche.'

So when, on Oaks Day at Epsom in the summer of 2007, a three-year-old colt called Escape Route dived out under the front of the starting stalls, John Gosden had no hesitation in dispatching it to what had become racing's, and indeed the wider equine community's, remedial home of choice.

Escape Route had done it before. He had also dived out of the front of the stalls at Newbury. He was a panicker, and very nervous: he had just got himself terrified of the stalls, so I thought the only thing was to get him used to them. At the end of the day, the stalls are just big steel cages, and if a horse gets a fright in them you can understand it not wanting to go near them at all.

So when Escape Route came to our place I put a set of hobbles on him and stood him by the stalls. It was not some 'whispering' magic: it was just some of the common sense I had learned from my 'de-flighting' work all the way back with Baltic Love and the clippers. If a horse is frightened of something you need to get him close to it, and show him he can't run away.

That's what we did with Escape Route: he had always been rushing at the stalls – what we were doing was slowing him down. He was only with us four or five days before we sent him back to John Gosden, who in those days was not far away at Manton. When the horse ran, I went to the start, got hold of him, and then led him across to stand next to the stalls. When the starter called the jockey's name I walked him into the stalls straight away, and stood in there with him to give some confidence. With a horse that had been rushing many people expected me to wait and go in at the last minute, but

Racing Post Saturday, October 6, 2007

1m1f Newmarket | live on C4 and RUK | Card and Spotlight, page 54

The man who put Escape Route back on straight and narrow

ESCAPE ROUTE, well fancied for today's Cambridgeshire, is lucky to be in the race. Lucky to be racing at all, actually.

The Elusive Quality colt lost the plot at Epsom on Oaks day, boiling over before the start of a Listed race and forcing his way out of the stalls, squeezing under the gate in his desperation. He had only been in the stalls for a matter of seconds, having been loaded last. Another starting-gate debacle followed at Newmarket, where he refused even to enter the stalls.

That event earned Escape Route a swift trip to the vet, where he became an Elusive Quality gelding, and then his trainer John Gosden took a tried-and-trusted course of action by sending him to Gary Witheford, an equine behaviourist based in Burbage, near Marlborough in Wiltshire, who had a reputation for soothing the most troubled of beasts.

Gosden dispatched the horse west with the instruction "take as long as you want to get him right", and settled down for a long wait. Four days later, the phone rang. It was Witheford. Escape Route was ready to come home.

Witheford, 47, has been 'fixing' problem horses for around 25 years, on and off, since his days as a groom with Stan Mellor in the time of Grand National third Royal Mail and Champion Hurdle second Pollardstown. He developed a reputation as someone who could handle the most difficult of equine recidivists, and although he later left racing, he then worked 'on the outside' in order to save the capital to start his own business dealing with horses.

Witheford, whose serene Noah's Ark of a homestead embraces dogs, hens, ducks, ferrets and a peacock, has also 'broken in' and ridden a veldt-fresh African zebra within 20 minutes – but that's another story. With 7,000 horses of all types through his hands in the last ten years, from Group 1 aces to children's ponies, Witheford's talents are widely recognised in all corners of the equine world, and the list of trainers who employ his services – both at his yard and at the races – reads like the index to *Horses in Training*.

"The horse is a flight animal, and I have to show him that I'm in charge, I'm the leader of the herd," he says. "I do this by controlling his movement with body language and eye contact, using a pressure and release technique.

"It all happens in minutes – I have to read it right straight away or I'll lose the horse."

He demonstrates his technique on Brujo, his white Andalucian stallion, who wheels and turns in the 50ft pen just as Escape Route did, gradually succumbing to Witheford's blend of challenging and coaxing and finally falling into line behind his 'leader'.

"Escape Route was one of the top five most difficult cases I've had to deal with," says Witheford. "But within three days, he was going through my set of stalls without a murmur.

"It's all about getting the horse's confidence back, and taking him to the stage where he wants to work for us again."

What they say about Gary Witheford

Roger Charlton
"There will always be a few difficult horses when it comes to the starting stalls, and without Gary's help a lot of them would be unable to run. Gary's work is a tremendous help in dealing with difficult characters. Being available to load difficult horses into the stalls at the races completes the work."

John Gosden
"He's a highly accomplished horseman who has great patience and knowledge in his approach to horses."

that would be trying to avoid the problem – I wanted to cure it. Escape Route won at Goodwood two races later, so I guess I did.

All this starting-stalls work can seem remote from the problems and issues you face with ordinary horses and ponies, but I don't think it is. The same principles apply, because all horses respond to the same language: what happens in the starting stalls can be an extreme form of behaviour, but the causes and the solutions are the same as you get with a pony that has suddenly got stroppy and doesn't want to go into the lorry, or rushes in and out of its box knocking everyone over.

You might think two of the biggest horses we were ever sent – Manet and Rodin, huge bay Percherons, really a French version of our Shire horses – would need a different treatment from racehorses, but in many ways what we did was the same as for the filly Step On Degas, who we got from Epsom when we were still in Wootton Bassett back in 1996. She was a typical, crazy two-year-old filly, eyes popping out of her head. They would tack her up, drive her to the gallops in the box, let her run and then drive her back again. We did lots of plastic and de-flighting work and walked her a lot, just to calm her down. She was fine by the time she left us.

So were Manet and Rodin. They were big buggers, mind. They were sent to us by Jonathan Miller, who used to write a very funny column in the *Sunday Times* called 'Mean Fields'. They were bolters – apparently they had run away and turned over the cart they were pulling, and somebody had been very badly hurt. And they had got very flighty. So we did The Points with them; we did all the plastic and de-flighting work; we opened umbrellas by them, threw down our 'shakers', even drove around them with a quad bike. In

The Percherons Manet and Rodin with us in 2004. Their owner wrote about it in the *Sunday Times*.

the end it was the same old thing: they had been spoilt; they had been allowed to take over; they didn't have a leader – they were thugs. Jonathan Miller got the idea: he called us a 'Boot Camp'. Well, we weren't harsh with them, but we had to show them who the leader was. He was sensible, too, because when they went back they were not put in a cart together straight away. If you have two horses who have been flighty, you have the obvious risk of them setting each other off again. So to start with, they were put in with a quieter horse to teach them manners.

Or take the rug we use to help horses that get touchy about bumping their flanks and quarters on the side of the starting stalls. The back of the rug is hooked to the stalls, the side padding protects them from the partition bars and, as the horse jumps away at the start, the rug stays put. The first thing like this was used by Jane Haddock to help one of her Arab horses that kept bumping its sides when it went into the horse walker. Monty Roberts first used his version back in 1992 on a colt of Mark Prescott's called Prince of Darkness, which then won a little race at Lingfield. The rugs became so popular that Monty marketed them around the world as the Monty Roberts Rug. It was a good idea but, looking back, actually quite obvious.

Originally I tried to stay away from using rugs at all: I think by wrapping horses up you are just putting a plaster on the problem. But way back in 1998 we had a horse called Choto Mate, the first we ever got from Richard Hannon, a leary two-year-old: we got him sorted using the Monty Roberts Rug, and then Richard Hughes won a race on him at Goodwood. But he was saying he was now jumping from the stalls slowly because of the rug, so I thought I ought to design something that was lighter and easier to remove.

My present one is a great improvement. Kingman can be a bit fidgety in the stalls, and for the 2,000 Guineas at Newmarket the Gosden team used their own big Monty Roberts-style rug for us to load him. It was a hot day, and the horse sweated so much under the rug that he was getting very tense before the gates opened. Three weeks later, at the Irish 2,000 Guineas, I loaded him with one of my rugs, and he didn't turn a hair.

When the sprinter Pivotal Point came to us in 2004 from Peter Makin, who trains at Ogbourne Maizey near Marlborough, he was one of the nastiest horses you could ever meet. He had been withdrawn for trying to wreck the stalls all three times he'd been to the races up north, and at York he'd made such a mess of himself that he'd had to be brought back in the horse ambulance. He wanted to kick the hell out of the stalls, and when he came here he wanted to kick the hell out of us. He was just a really bad-tempered horse, who needed to be taught that we could disarm him. I laid him down in the ring and sat on him. Then I put padding on the back gates of the stalls all the way down to the floor so he could not get his hocks beneath them, put him in, and just let him kick. When he finally realised he was not going to get away with it, he gave up. He became OK: he was a normal horse and a good one. He won six races for Peter Makin, including the Stewards' Cup at Goodwood in 2004.

In 2005, when the new Steriline stalls were brought in from Australia, many of the problems were not the horses' fault – for, whatever the authorities said up in London, these stalls were not the same as the ones we had trialled up at Wolverhampton in the winter. These ones were like tin cans, and as soon as one horse kicked, the whole thing began to rattle, and then the other horses started going off. They also had bars lower down on the back gates which made the horses kick, and unpadded ledges against the sides which made horses flinch.

I got involved very early on, because I was dealing with a horse called Envision. He was the first one to kick off at Newmarket, which had used these new Steriline stalls for the first time that April. Envision, one of Julie Wood's horses trained by Richard Hannon, went berserk in the stalls and broke the leg of a handler called Lofty who never fully recovered. At home we got Envision sorted, and he would go into our stalls without a problem, but when we took him to Newbury for a practice session, they had the Steriline stalls with the low bars, and he kicked the hell out of them again, and injured himself.

It was so stupid: the back gate of the stalls was three panels lower, so when a horse went in, he could feel the panel below his hocks, and he would start kicking like crazy. Envision made a real mess of his legs – the vet's bills must have been horrendous. We patched him up and got him right, and then they only ran him at tracks that didn't have the Steriline stalls. He got his confidence back and won five races in a row.

Soon after Envision I had this real good filly of Gerard Butler's called Tarfah: she was a decent mare, and later became the dam of the Derby winner Camelot. She kicked off really badly at Newbury, and I remember leading her back with her hind legs all bleeding. I told the guys in charge this was a disgrace, but they just said, 'The stalls are the same as in Dubai.' I told them they were not – they were like tin cans, and had no padding, and that they should rubberise the jockeys' standing bars so there would not be cold, bare metal against the horse's skin. At that stage nobody would have had Steriline stalls of their own, so even if their horses were walking in fine at home, it was a whole new ball game at the races. This was when John Gosden said, 'We need a meeting,' and a whole lot of us met up at Newbury: jockeys, trainers, handlers.

Then we went up to the BHA in London. Mark Johnston was there, as was Chris Wall, the trainers' chairman, Richard Hills, Gosden himself, one of the Hannons and several others. We got the BHA to agree to raise the stalls, rubberise those standing bars and take off the bottom of the three bars at the back, to make them the same as the other sets of stalls. They also started soundproofing them to stop all the rattle, and slowly we began to have fewer problems. It took a while, because they could only do one set of stalls at a time, but at least it did not cost as much as it might have done, because one of the trainers at the meeting was Rod Millman, and when the BHA said it would all be very expensive and they would need to get someone over from Australia, Rod said, 'That's a load of *******s: my father has a fabricating business, and he would do it for half the cost.'

The authorities are much more reasonable nowadays, but sometimes they still find it very hard to listen. In one week I had three cases of a horse kicking out, and getting his hind leg wedged up behind him on the back of the ledge where the jockeys put their feet. I explained that we needed to slope that ledge, so a horse's hoof could slide back to the ground. They said, 'Oh, we will have to ask Steriline in Australia.' 'No we don't,' I told them. 'I'm putting horses in the stalls every day, and I'm telling you we need to change this.' They said they'd come back to me: four weeks later I was still waiting.

The stalls handlers do a good job, and I get on well with them. But too often they are having to try and heave horses in which the trainers have not taught properly. If you are calm and firm from the beginning, and let horses take their time – let them sniff the side of the gates and wonder what it's all about – most horses will load quite easily, and as they are first-time learners, you should not have a problem on the racecourse. But some trainers and their riders make a big performance of it all: everyone gets tense, the horse picks this up, and reacts badly. You may have to be firm and persistent, but you can't do it with muscle – the horse weighs half a ton. You are never going to win physically. We get our horses to back off, and then follow us by checking them on the head collars: Pressure and Release, of course. And if you watch, almost always we lead our horses into the stalls without a pusher.

We also take them in without what we think is one of the best and simplest encouragements of all: 'the tappers'. It gets my goat that the BHA won't allow them. They are three-foot-long-modified lunge whips with which we literally tap the horse on the quarters from either side when he is at the back of the stalls. At home we use them all the time – it is literally a tap to encourage them forward: never a whack. If you whack a horse it will kick out and resist: this is just a tap to encourage it forward into the face of the guy in front of it with the halter. Yet the BHA won't allow our 'tappers' because they don't want anyone to see sticks being used down at the start.

It's ridiculous. Every day you will see four, five, six handlers heaving half a ton of resisting horse into the stalls, when with a couple of tappers behind them on either side you can encourage them forward straight and quick. I hate having horses hit, but a tap at the right time can only help. Last year all one of ours wanted was a tap, and so I put Ryan Moore's whip under my arm, gave it a tap, and handed it back to him. If he had hit it he would have been suspended. The BHA are making rules to please people who don't understand horses. It's stupid.

Trainers now understand getting horses into stalls a lot better, but the odd one is still a disgrace. Not long ago this guy up north got three or four handlers to help him put something through the stalls for a practice. They got down there and this guy – some say he is a good trainer, but not me – puts a twitch on the horse. But it won't go anywhere, so he starts to lose his temper: he takes the twitch off its nose, and starts beating it with the twitch handle, which is made like a truncheon. Eventually they get it into the stalls, and then he gets up above it and starts beating it again. It's bleeding from its head, and he is hitting it and yelling, 'You ****ing bastard' and all the rest. The horse came out, but the stalls handlers were so sickened they just walked away.

For a young horse, for any horse, the inside of the starting stalls can be an alarming place: anyone in there with them needs to give them confidence, because if they flip, it can be very dangerous. It certainly was with a filly of Andrew Balding's called Sabah: at home she had been fine, but when she went to run at Newbury she went berserk in the stalls, and had to be withdrawn. That's when we were called in. She gave me the most frightening time I have ever had on a racecourse.

The moment she arrived you could see she was in a bad way. She was sweating so much she was scorching the grass beneath her. We were with her for two hours, and eventually got her in using a hood and a rug. We thought we had cracked it – only for her to suddenly rear up and crack her head on the beam. There was blood everywhere. She was off for five or six months while they rebuilt her skull with chicken wire.

She came home to us at Westcourt, but was still dodgy, and on one occasion reared up and knocked Craig out – he was only 19 then. It was at that point I said, 'She's a well-bred filly: let her go off and be a mother.' But Andrew and his assistant Chris Bonner had designed a head cap for her a bit like that worn by Petr Cech, the Chelsea goalkeeper, and they wanted to persevere. Finally we thought we had cured her, and went with her for her first race at Windsor. We put a hood on her, and I led her in smooth enough, but once in the stall she panicked and threw herself on the ground, with me trapped beneath her. 'What do we do now, Gary?' asked Judy Grange, the starter. 'Well, I have got two options,' I said. 'Either I try and get out and leave her, or I pull off the blindfold and hope she gets up without breaking me.'

So I gradually eased the blind off one eye, and she looked at me, and slowly got to her feet, leaving me to slip out the front. She ran well that day, better the next, won the third time and was then placed in a Listed race. John Gosden is right: the starting stalls are the most dangerous part of flat racing, but handling horses in them is a challenge I like. It teaches you to read a horse's body language, because your life might depend on it. It has taught me a lot, and introduced me to many people. I have met quite a few horses that could be classed as criminals – but I've met some champions, too.

'Going into the winner's circle was very special for me. Horses had brought me a long, long way.'

15 | Sea The Stars

On Tuesday 13 October 2009 I was at John Oxx's Currabeg stable in Kildare, to interview the extraordinary team behind the Derby winner Sea The Stars. This magnificent-looking three-year-old had just rounded off the unique sequence of winning a Group One race every month from May to October, ending with France's Prix de l'Arc de Triomphe nine days earlier. His support team were unfailingly pleasant and inspiring, and there was one of them I had never met before: Gary Witheford.

Meeting him came at the end of a pretty long day. Even John Oxx's customarily professorial calm had broken down momentarily as he described the moment at Epsom when Mick Kinane took the saddle off Sea The Stars and whispered, 'This is one of the greats.' Everyone from stable lad to stud manager had their tribute to pay, but just as we were packing up John said, 'The farm is only ten minutes away: if you could get up there you could see the guy who broke him.' It was one of the best tips I was ever given.

For by 2009 I was the sort of racing bag-carrier who thought he had seen it all. I had been a jockey, a TV presenter, a writer and, if you really want to know, had once ridden The Unrideable Mule at Bertram Mills' Circus. I had travelled the racing globe from Beverley to Buenos Aires, and had the swank to write a book about it. I had ridden thoroughbreds over fences at Aintree, and Akal Tekkes up sand dunes in Turkmenistan. I had watched some very poor horsemen as well as some supremely gifted ones. I didn't think I was in for too many surprises. I was wrong.

For what I saw over the next hour that autumn evening in Kildare was more than a revelation. It appeared to challenge the normal rules of horsemanship, while at the same time being no more than crashing common sense. Gary was not some equitational intellectual with a new line in psychobabble: he had been a stable lad with my friend and rather superior rival Stan Mellor, the first jockey to ride 1,000 jumping winners. Just one hundred was all I could manage.

*But Gary's no-nonsense approach was a million miles from the harsh and sometimes sadistic 'Come here you ****er' line to which too many stable hands have often resorted. He was direct and firm, but fair to the point of familiar. He wasn't claiming 'gifts', and tried to disown the term 'whisperer'. What he had was years of experience using a language of touch, eye contact and body movement embedded in the psyche of the horse and other animals of flight. Right in front of my eyes, Gary transformed the time taken for 'breaking-in' a yearling from the standard weeks to less than half an hour. Sea The Stars had taken just 12 minutes.*

At the end of the process the riders stood high on their horses' backs. To me it seemed as if Gary was standing truth on its head. I had thought I knew everything, and he had knocked me cold. My only saving grace was that two years earlier someone as wise and sensible as John Oxx had been knocked cold too.

Timarwa was the very best of the best of the Aga Khan's breeding. She was by his superstar Daylami out of Timarida, whom John Oxx had trained to win ten races for the Aga, including Group Ones in Ireland, France, Germany, America and Canada. Both sire and dam were grey; Timarwa wasn't, but she had talent. If only she would agree to use it.

She was a three-year-old with classic potential, but she wouldn't go anywhere near the stalls: just planted herself, and swung herself from side to side like fillies do. She had refused to go in at Leopardstown. John Oxx would not have known me from Joe Bloggs but he had been told about me by Eddie Harty Jnr, for whom I had sorted out a real bitch of a mare. John said, 'We've got this filly who is very difficult, but we think a lot of her. Could you come over?'

John is a very nice man, but he is a big player, and for me this was quite a challenge: whenever I get on the plane to go to new places I feel physically sick. I don't eat; I don't drink; and when I begin working I often feel quite faint. Once I've done the job I'm OK, but it's the nervous anticipation. It has always been a problem, which made trying to work with people and do demos so difficult, and that's why Cozy Powell had to push me so hard at the beginning.

So I got to John Oxx's some time during second lot, about half past ten. On the box doors there were brass plaques with the names of the champions that had stood there before – something great had been in Timarwa's box. She wasn't the best-looking of horses – dark brown and quite narrow – but she had a lovely head on her: a typical Aga Khan filly. They had the starting stalls out at the back of the barn, so I just put my rope halter on her and did a bit of my Pressure and Release work, checking her and sending her back. I spent a minute, maybe a minute and a half, and then she walked into the stalls behind me without any hassle. Because she had failed to go in at Leopardstown she needed an official stalls test, so they rang up the starter and we took her across to a set of stalls on the Curragh – and she walked in without a bother. They had been trying with rugs and blinds and everything, so they were good and impressed.

A lot of the Irish, they get stuck in their ways: 'Well, this is how it's done, and that's it.' But although these lads were old, they wanted to learn. They watched Timarwa stopping when I stopped, and walking when I walked, and when I did that classic thing where I stop the horse, tie a knot in the lead rope and leave it there, they went, 'Wow.' There was this three- or four-hundred-thousand-pound horse, it's stood in the middle of the yard on its own with just a halter hanging to the floor: the extra weight on that lead rope was enough to anchor her. It showed, I explained, just how sensitive horses were.

John's very quiet, a thinking man; his son Kevin was also there, and the assistant Slim O'Neill, and Jeff Houlihan whom you used to see at the races. They were very interested, and soon it was, 'Could you have a look at this one? Could you have a look at that one?' Instead of one horse I ended up looking at five or six, and we had a sort of mini demo, and next minute I had got a couple of the lads out and put the halters on them like I do with people: 'This is how it feels.'

Then there was this big grey horse: 'he just won't let us get on him,' said John. 'Well', I said, 'there's only one way to sort this. Put a saddle and bridle on it, take it into the barn, and I will put it on the floor for you. I promise,' I said, 'you'll get on it, and you won't have a problem with it again.' 'Really?' 'Yes' – and I went in there with this big grey horse. I didn't have all my stuff, so I borrowed a stirrup leather and tied its near fore up, put a lunge line over its shoulder and round its tail, pulled its head towards me, and laid it down on the floor. I got the lad to sit on it and walk all over it. 'Right, now let's get it up.' I untied the strap, put the jockey on, and it was perfect. The boy rode it round the indoor school and out into the trotting ring, and it wasn't a problem. It was never a problem again.

'What else do you do?' said John Oxx, and I told him that I broke in yearlings, so he took me down to his farm where he broke his, and told me how they did it the traditional way over three or four weeks, with plenty of long-reining. So I said I only took twenty minutes, and while I long-rein them I only do that for two or three minutes, just round to the left and round to the right. He sat there very quiet, taking it all in, and then said, 'Let's have a look at you coming over. I will run it past Pat Downes [the Aga Khan's racing manager] and see how we get on.'

I was back a fortnight later when Timarwa ran for the first time. I brought Suze with me and thought we would make a weekend of it, but before the race I began to get nervous. I said to her, 'We've got the taxi outside: if this horse doesn't go in the stalls, for God's sake get down to the mile-and-a-quarter start, pick me up, and we'll get out of Ireland quick.' She laughed her head off, and luckily it didn't come to that. The filly walked straight in, and won easy. Then she was fourth in the Irish Oaks, and won a Listed race at Gowran Park. I loaded her in all her races except the last one, which was in the Breeders Cup at Monmouth Park, New York, but I did take her to the airport to make sure she got on the plane.

The main reason I couldn't go to New York was because John Oxx had got us over to do the yearlings. On the first day I must have started at about 8 o'clock and John did not come down until around 9.30, by which time we would have already broken three or four. He came with his son Kevin and his wife Caitriona, and Pat Downes was there, too. So it happened that the first yearling they saw was a colt by Cape Cross out of the mare Urban Sea, who had herself won the Arc de Triomphe and been the dam of the Derby-winner Galileo. But whatever his breeding, this was a stunner. I don't think he had a name back then. He did later. They called him Sea The Stars.

What we did with him was the same as we do for all horses starting out, whether they are ponies, thoroughbreds or one of Brujo's progeny. They all come into the ring with just a head collar on, and the first thing I do is to put a lunge line on them and shoo them away. Yes, literally throw the lunge line at them and then I can see if I have got flight. As I have kept saying, a horse is a flight animal, so you have to encourage that flight, and then harness it. Shoo something like Sea The Stars and he will canter away at once. Some might be a bit more reluctant; the worst are the ones who have been spoilt or hand-reared, because they have lost a lot of their flight. But in the ring you can almost always get them going with just the end of the lunge line – no whip or yelling or anything: just be direct and dominant in your body language.

That first canter tells me which way he prefers to go: either left rein or right rein. They normally go away to the right – but say they do: when I come to put the jockey on later I will make sure he goes to the left. That first canter also tells me how much he is listening to me. A horse like Sea The Stars would have been doing it straight away – you can see it because he will have his inside ear bent back to look and listen: his ear is locked-on.

After a couple of circuits, sometimes even sooner, he will start moving his mouth and lowering his head. As you know, I call it 'lick and chew', and they will start doing this even at the fast trot or canter, and lower their head. That means they are passive: prepared to accept what I want them to do next. So I step back, drop my eyes, and invite them to turn and come in towards me. When they do, I then shoo them off in the other direction, and we do the same thing.

After they have done a couple of circuits the other way and come in, they are ready for the saddle. For once they have 'flighted' both ways they have given me something back: they have told me how they are likely to take it. I will have seen whether this is a nervous colt, or a nervous filly that may be frightened or aggressive to you when the saddle is put on, or whether they are just a run-of-the-mill horse just happy to go along with it all. This is where eye contact is very important. When they have gone passive you must drop your eyes, so they realise you are not a threat to them. You have rewarded them for accepting you as leader.

So I have the saddle and pad brought in, and put down in front of them to smell. Sea The Stars just lowered his head and smelled it, and said, 'Oh, I don't mind that – I can smell the other horses on it.' But with the nervous ones you need to hold the pad and saddle up to their noses for them to smell: they need to understand. Then you put the pad and saddle on them, do the girth up – and then they will explode. Not all of them, but I would say 60 or 70%.

I just stand back and let them do what they want to do: buck, buck, buck. Most of them won't buck more than a couple of circuits, but at this point I pick up the Long Tom, because you do have to watch out for yourself. Some of them will turn and come at you – the fillies are usually the worst. They have accepted you as their leader, and now all of a sudden they feel something odd on their back and around their belly, and they explode and want to come to you for help. They are bucking and fly-jumping like broncos and God knows what, so you've got to be very careful and side-step. That's when, if I need to, I'll slap them behind the hocks with the Long Tom so they're not jumping on top of me.

Remember, they still only have a head collar and a lunge line on their heads, but after their bit of bucking I bring them in and put a bridle on them. This will have the ordinary reins which the rider will use later, but I also attach a pair of long reins, dropping them over the side and threading them through the stirrup irons, which are tied together under the horse's belly with a neck strap to prevent them flapping around. Then I step back and flick the long reins, and the horse will walk forward. The odd nervous one, especially a filly, will lash out at the feeling of the long rein close to its backside, but I don't take the rein away. I keep flicking it at her, and suddenly she will stop doing that and start walking normally, and not with her legs

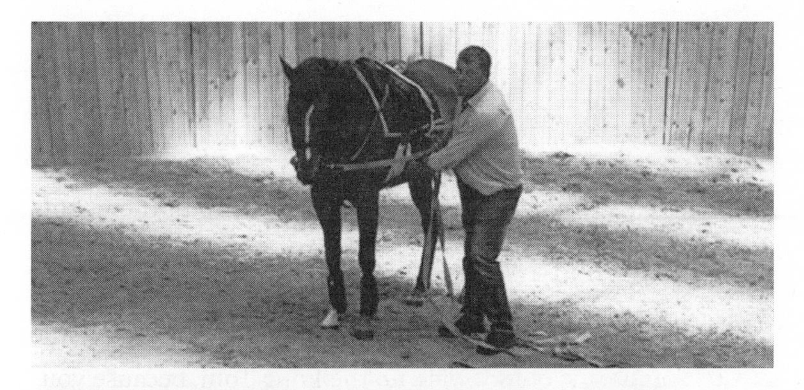

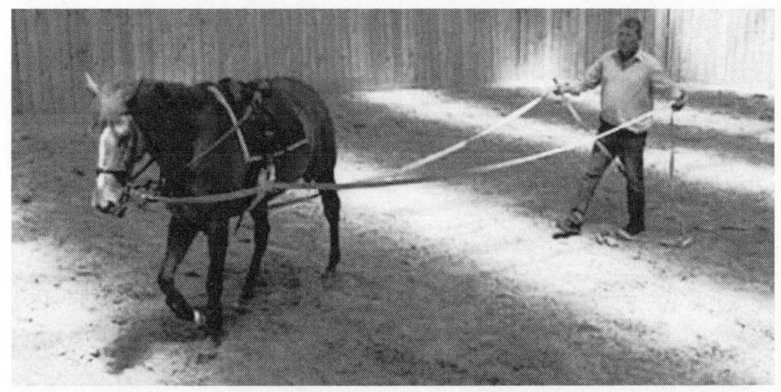

From top: Tacked-up, long reined, rider on board.

tucked all tight under her backside. Then it's the first turn, and this is important.

If I am going round clockwise – that is, on the right rein – what I do is pull the right rein towards me to get the horse off the wall, and so give it some space to turn in against the wall: always turn in, never out. Then I release the right rein, and apply the pressure on the left rein, and step my body across behind it. Now I am opening a door for it to the left like I do in The Points. It moves naturally to the left and through that 'door', and it has made its first turn. Then you take it round in the other direction, and do the same thing the other way. When you have done those two things you have a good idea of how you are going. With Sea The Stars I was saying, '**** me – we've only been going five minutes, and we are almost there already.'

Then what I do is slowly gather up the long reins, and move my body closer in behind the horse so I am driving it – maybe for a circuit – just at the walk. The horse will naturally walk, but if you've got a colt or a filly that is trying to bolt, the more you turn it, the quicker it will stop, and suddenly it is walking easily. In the traditional way you drive them like this for days and weeks to 'give them a mouth'. But a horse has 'a mouth' already – he showed it to you when he made those turns on the long rein. He is a first-time learner: walking him up the roads is wasting his time and yours.

His 'mouth' is only going to be as good as the person at the end of the rein. In the old method of 'breaking' you were meant to keep a pressure on both sides of the bit, even when you were turning the horse. To me this just means that you are giving two instructions at the same time: if you want to go round to the right, you put pressure on the right rein but ease off on the left, so the animal is only getting one message. As they're first time learners you don't want to muddle them. So when I have turned him left and right into the wall, I turn him into the centre of the ring, walk him a few strides, and then put a bit of pressure on the bit to halt him, so he has to stop dead when I ask him. He has accepted saddle and bridle, and been driven both ways and into the centre of the ring. He has walked, and turned, and stopped. I count up to ten in my head, and then ask him to come back two strides for me. When he does, that's it: he's ready to be ridden.

The rider comes in with his eyes down, because that is a passive movement: he doesn't want to have his head up with a look that says, 'I am going to master you.' I unclip the offside long rein, and clip the nearside one to the coupling between the two rings of the bit. Remember this, because in a minute or two it will be important. I rattle the rein on the coupling so the horse is looking at me, but I have it loose, not like the 'get-a-tight-hold-of-the-******'s-head' way of the old days, with three or four people almost pinning the horse down. That's like me grabbing you by the throat. Everything is loose, but we are concentrating.

After the jockey has untied the strap holding the stirrup irons together and then buckles it back round the horse's neck, I grab his leg and lift him. The rider does not jump: it's a smooth, quiet lift, not the jerk of a jump. That's important, too, for the rider is lifted up to be lying not on the saddle, with any weight on it yet, but with his or her belly-button across the wither in front of the saddle. At that stage a few of the horses will scatter away, but only a few – say five or six out of a hundred. But if it happens, there is no shouting: you just bring it back to where you were in the pen, and go through it again. The rider is lying there like a piece of meat, and I'm holding the horse with my eye and body contact, just as I was when I was putting that saddle on his back and the bridle in his mouth. I have his head bent in to the left, and then I walk backwards and bring him towards me for three, five, maybe even seven strides.

We need to be in the centre, because if the horse does rush, the rider doesn't want to be thrown into the side railings, as he is lying across the wither in a vulnerable position, with his own head hanging over the other side of the saddle. Because I've got the horse's head turned in towards me, it can't see the person lying behind on the other side, and it's only after it has walked a few strides, and I can see that the horse's back is down and accepting the weight, that I will turn its head straight and its right eye will see the rider's head. If a horse is going to jump, that's when he'll do it, and the occasional one will panic. In which case what we do is to put on a pair of blinkers, meaning the horse can see forwards, but backward vision is shut out by the eye-cups. Last summer we had a two-year-old sent to us that was completely unrideable until we did this. People in racing see blinkers as a 'hurry-up' aid, but really they are a pacifier: you put them on a horse with a cart precisely to stop it worrying about what is happening behind.

At the moment we only put blinkers on the odd horse, and take them off once it has accepted being ridden. But there is a good case for making it standard – Craig is doing it more and more. It means the horse is only having one pressure at a time: It can then feel the weight of the rider on its back without having to worry at the sight of the human up behind. Once it is happy being ridden, you can take the blinkers off, and away you go.

Now we have got to get the rider into the saddle. This stage shouldn't take very long, and there is a good reason why: for while horses – especially young horses like we had at John Oxx's – are first-time learners, there is only a short window of attention for them to receive the lesson and move on. So I stand in front of the horse, and reach across with my right hand to put the rider's toe into the left-hand stirrup, while he holds hard onto the off-side stirrup with his own right hand, and then levers his body and leg over to put his right-hand toe into that stirrup. I have the horse's head turned in towards me to protect that back eye line, but I make sure I also have the rider's head over the near side of the neck, so I can drag him off into me if anything happens.

The rider has now got his toes in the irons, but his backside is in the air to keep the weight off the horse's back. I walk forward towards me for twenty or thirty seconds before he lowers his backside into the saddle. Some horses will then explode, but it is very rare. Under the old way we used to expect almost 70% to explode when you sat on them – after all those weeks of putting rollers and cruppers and martingales on them, teaching them to buck. Now it is one in a hundred. Well, if my way works for 99 but not for one, which is the right way?

But the rider sits right forward, not back in the saddle, so the weight is on the horse's shoulder, and once he's settled I step aside and throw the lunge line at the horse to encourage him to run away, as I taught him to at the beginning. I make that kissing sound to press him on, and within about four or five strides at the trot, I'll get the horse into the canter. In the old way it was walk, walk, long before you trotted, let alone cantered. All you were doing was putting lessons off, and getting the horse fitter and less easy to manage.

At this stage, if the horse does want to run, I encourage my riders to let it run. It's important not to panic: they're not bucking, they're just running away from you on their back. So you let them run for maybe half a circuit, and then ease them back so they feel the pressure of the bit: you've already taught them to come back from pressure on the bit when you were long-reining them and halting them. The one thing you must not do is to start yanking them back – and anyway, if they do bolt in the ring they can't go anywhere. You do get nervous colts, but it is usually the fillies: they're the ones that teach you to ride. After a bit the colts are usually, 'Oh OK, OK, I'll do it.' It's my whole theory on horses: you tell a colt; you ask a filly.

Of course, you need a good rider who understands what you are trying to do, but once the reins are tightened and eased, the horses usually come back very quickly. It's natural for them to flight and come back, and when you are satisfied that they are cantering all right, you tell the rider to 'unclip'. He will lean forward and unclip the lead rein from the coupling, and it will fall away like a tow-line from a glider. The pilot is on his own!

Then I come out – literally run out of the ring – and that's when we use the felt padded sticks, because when I come out, 90% of the horses want to stop. It's my body that's been chasing them forward round the ring and driving them in the long reins; then all of a sudden this leader has gone, and the horse is saying, 'What the **** has happened here? Why has he left me?' The sticks don't hurt them, and we always use them on the rump, behind the saddle. But they make a noise, and they encourage the horse to go on, to realise it has to answer to the man on top. After a couple of circuits we get back to a walk and

Horses are first time learners and our yearlings are usually happily ridden away within 30 minutes.

This isn't posing. We do it at the end of every 'starting' session because it gets the horse to accept something way above his eyeline. That can become vital when he goes into the stalls.

the riders turn them into the fence – because if you turn them the other way it's as if you are opening the door for them to go anywhere they want. If they are going to bolt or buck you are showing them that open space to run into: turn them into the fence and their path is tight. As long as they turn twice each way, I'm happy. Then we take him into the centre: I come back into the pen, clip on that lunge line again, and get the jockey to get off, on, off, on, maybe three or four times, so the horse doesn't flight. The jockey's now being legged up properly like he's going to be legged up for the rest of his life.

Then I'll say to the jockey, 'Stand up,' and he'll stand up on the saddle – right up. I'm positioned in front of the horse, because it respects me and won't jump forward into me. Then the jockey jumps off. He literally jumps off from on top of the saddle – jumps, and the horse never moves. This isn't a posing thing: it's much more than that – it means the horse has accepted someone up above his eyeline. If he is going to be a racehorse and there is an incident in the stalls, the handlers will jump up into the rigging and lots of horses that have never seen men up above them will start to panic. Mine don't: they learned that the very first day.

Craig and I now 'break' – we do need another word – 'start' 500–600 yearlings like this. Anyone can do it – a lad who worked for me does all of Richard Hannon's – provided everything is straightforward, but if you run into a problem, that is when expertise is important – the difference, if you like, between a mechanic and a technician. Craig is very good, and can do most things on his own, but if there's a problem with a difficult horse he will call me over.

That first trip to John Oxx's was a great time. There were all these new people: among the riders was Cathy Gannon, who was supposed to be off with a damaged shoulder, but after two days she said, 'Let me on, let me on!', and loved it. It was fascinating for all the lads, because here were the yearlings going round, and within half an hour they were ridden away, and we were standing on their backs.

But Sea The Stars was stunning: you couldn't fault him. He was a really good masculine prototype. When Craig got off him, he said to me, 'Dad, this is some horse. He's so intelligent; he's so light on his feet – and he learns so quickly.' It had been amazing to watch – within minutes he was doing twists and turns and 'changing legs' as though he had been ridden for months. 'This is the best yearling I have ever sat on,' Craig said. 'I don't know if he will be any good as a racehorse, but what a brain!'

But he did turn out to be a racehorse – and what a racehorse! What he did as a three-year-old was quite unbelievable. Before the Derby John Oxx rang, and said, as an insurance policy would I go to the start with the horse? Sea The Stars walked

Sea The Stars wins the Derby.

into the stalls good as gold, and I got a lift back listening to the race in the starter's car. Going into that Epsom winner's circle was very special for me, for here was a horse I had been part of just as I had been with Alpenstock, when I led him in at the Cheltenham Festival back in 1977. Horses had brought me a long, long way.

'People were frightened of him – and he became frightened of what they might do to him.'

16 | Winston and the Future

By most standards Gary Witheford is a huge success. He has a fine yard in a beautiful setting, and is a figure of increasing renown both in racing and the wider equine world. But he remains tormented by his past and troubled by his future: such angst is both his driving force and weakest link.

Not for him the senior statesman status of 79-year-old Monty Roberts and his global organisation 'Join-Up International' with the Queen as its patron. Nor yet the Zen-like calm of Buck Brannaman as he takes his own clinics across the States and as far afield as Australia and New Zealand. Gary Witheford remains a more pressurised individual, endlessly burning up the motorways to fire-fight problems in the starting stalls, while trying to fit in remedial work with equine misfits back at home.

At 54, two years older than Brannaman, Gary is getting dangerously long in the tooth for those risk-packed cages on the racecourse, and yet finds it difficult to find competent deputies beyond his son Craig. Difficult, too, is the delegation needed during all those hours on the road. Suzanne Witheford has brought remarkable order into his schedule, but the ever-increasing demand for his starting-stalls service makes the original yard-based concept even harder to run.

Part of this is down to his own restless temperament, on which early abuse and lack of appreciation have left wounds that can never heal. It is surely no coincidence that both Roberts and Brannaman were also abused in childhood, although in their cases by tyrannical fathers, not scheming paedophiles who are still at large. But Gary's other difficulty lies with the built-in conservatism of the British horse world, where the basic tenets of Natural Horsemanship are still viewed with a degree of suspicion, if not slightly comic contempt.

This could leave Gary as an isolated maverick raging against the equine establishment, be it the received wisdom on spurs, snaffle bits, stalls 'tappers' or the insidious use of tranquilisers for everything from clipping to riding out. It would be more than a shame if that were to happen, because the work he has done and the knowledge he has absorbed are both remarkable and unique. His Natural Horsemanship may derive from the original ways of the cowboys out west, but the development of them is his own, and once understood can greatly improve our handling and understanding of horses.

For his rage is most of all on their behalf, and is a rejection both of the long-perpetuated cruelties of the past, and the hypocritical anthropomorphism of the present, which wants to treat animals as humans while also putting them on the dinner plate. Beneath that still vigorous exterior there is something of the old carter's wisdom: wanting always to be kind to his horse, but knowing that the best way to help him pull the wagon is to clear his head, not give him the vote.

From the evidence of my own eyes and many hours in his company, it must be to riders', and especially to horses', benefit that such lessons always be remembered. Let's hope this book can be the start, not the finish, of that process. Not for nothing is our title If Horses Could Talk. *For if it were so, one of their first words to Gary Witheford would be: 'Thank you.'*

Winston was a bolter. As soon as they tried to get a leg on him, he would bronco off and bury them. He came to us this year. He was a magnificent-looking horse – a fine big bay warmblood, and must have been at least 16.2. He was only five years old and this lady, Amanda Gillett, had bought him to develop into a decent dressage horse. Amanda had ridden for 40 years and is no mug, but this was a classic case of how things can go wrong with a horse.

He had gone to a professional yard to be broken, and they got him ridden to some extent, but mostly walking and trotting rather than getting on with the job. And they had not cured the broncing: when he came back to his owner in Essex, he first buried the owner's sister and broke her ribs. He was diagnosed with ulcers; went to another trainer. But when Amanda finally got on him, he flew off with her and did her in too, breaking her arm.

She had him booked in for the big sleep, but found our name on the internet, and Suzanne told her either I would fix him or he would be unfixable. Amanda says what happened then was a miracle: it wasn't – it's what we do. For straight away you could see the problem. He had been getting away with things: he was a big young horse and people had become frightened of him, and he had become frightened of what they might do to him – I think they had even put a dummy in the saddle so that no one would get hurt. That only makes it worse, and in any case, it's just avoiding the problem, just as it is if you use [the tranquiliser] ACP. Of course you can quieten a horse if you dope it – but what happens when you don't?

It's amazing, and I'd say scandalous, how often people use ACP today. In racing, trainers use it to get their horses in the stalls, and although it's against the rules, they even do it to pass a stalls test, as that very rarely has a dope test. That's really stupid, because when it actually runs it won't be tranquilised, and so the stalls handlers at the start get the problem. But even more shocking is the number of horses given ACP before going out to exercise. I have even known cases of stable lads and girls stealing tablets so they can have a quieter ride in the morning. No one ever did this when I was at Stan Mellor's, and anyway, how can a horse be properly, or safely, galloped if it is on tranquilisers? Do the owners know?

Winston was not on ACP, but he did need sorting. He was all right loose in the ring, but once he had someone on him he was wild. So I decided to do the two things I do with all buckers and plungers. The first was to tie his near fore up; the second was to put our 'bronco buster' on to his bridle. What we do is get a long piece of normal binder twine – let's say three metres long – tie a loop at the end, and then thread it down under the horse's gum and up between its ears, before taking it back down through the rings of the bit, criss-cross it over its neck, and tie it to the saddle like you do with grass reins.

I got the idea from watching kids with binder-twine 'grass reins' on their ponies. Without any help the little kid would just be dragged over the front every time the pony reaches down to take a bit of grass. But if you attach the pony's bit to the side of the saddle with binder twine, all is rosy. What's more, there is no need to pull at the pony at all: it is all on the saddle. In the same way, with our binder-twine attachment, if a horse like Winston puts its head down to try and buck, he will be putting pressure on himself. Doing all that plunging is habit-forming, so you have to get them out of it, and while this looks quite severe I have never had a horse hurt itself with it. He is only going to have a real go once, although you may need to make him try. We certainly had to with Winston.

For when we put our rider on his back, you could see that the horse wanted to get rid of him, but with his leg tied up was not quite sure how to do it. So we made him try. The rider had a padded whip, and he smacked and kicked Winston forward. You would be amazed how much a horse can do on three

Nika trying to put Jason on to Winston that first day.

Minutes after this, Winston was working with us, not against us.

legs, and you can see how angry he was as he plunged forward. When they are angry that top lip goes all stiff – I call it 'the elephant trunk'. But Winston couldn't put his head down because of the binder twine, and because of that he could not even try and buck, although with only one foreleg to balance on anyway it would have been a pretty bad idea.

He did a whole circuit like that. Amanda Gillett was almost choking in horror, but I told her to trust me. We undid the foreleg, and Winston trotted round sensibly. We undid the binder twine, and he was the beautiful mover he was bred to be. This time Amanda was choking with tears, and in Winston's language he was telling us he was fine. He has never bucked since. We kept him for four days, working in the ring and hacking around the lanes with other horses, and sent him back to her. A couple of months later he came back to us for a refresher, because Amanda had been away and rather spooked herself the first time she got on him again, but this time he didn't need any leg tie or binder twine.

She is still determined to make him into a decent dressage horse, and there is no reason why she shouldn't, because she is being sensible about it. So many people 'over-horse' themselves, and then try and get all sorts of gadgets to compensate, when the real problem is their own lack of experience or ability – usually both. Not everyone can be a brilliant rider, so it's no good buying a horse to do things you can't manage, because you won't enjoy it. It's like going down a black run if you are not a good skier: you are only going to frighten yourself. Then people come to me saying they have 'horse problems'. I have to explain to them that their horse has a 'people problem' – them!

But I don't think they are helped by what they are told are the right things to use. Take the snaffle bit: in Joe Public's eyes this is the kindest of bits for a horse's mouth, but I assure you it's probably one of the worst. Try it on your own hand: you'll see it has a sort of nutcracker action – imagine that going into the roof of a horse's mouth. *Ouch.* I use what are called Myler bits. Try that on your hand, and you'll see it has a link in the centre, which means it is shaped for the mouth and also twists back and forth: when you pull on the rein the bit doesn't go up into the roof of the mouth – it stays where it is. It twists at a different angle.

But snaffle bits are nothing compared to spurs, or those thin dressage whips that can easily cut a horse's skin if you hit hard enough. It's a joke that people can make a fuss about the use of padded whips on racehorses, and yet in showjumping and dressage they use spurs all the time – Craig's girlfriend Nika, competes a nice Connemara, had a judge tell her she would not be able to progress any further unless she wore spurs. So the authorities are officially encouraging the use of spurs. Just think of the difference: being hit on the rump by a heavily padded whip, or jabbed in the ribs by a not-always-blunt piece of stainless steel. It may not be popular, but I am sticking to my guns about this. You don't have to hurt horses. I don't see any rhyme or reason in it at all.

People just don't want to read a horse's language. I did a demo many years ago at Hartpury College, just outside Gloucester. There was this big dressage horse that some 'Sally-Anne's' parents had bought her for £50,000, and it kept rearing and bucking and rearing and bucking. I took this horse on in the College's massive indoor school, and it was the best I had ever worked at that time: a beautiful horse, a beautiful gelding, big bay and striking-looking. It did The Points work straight away; it Called-Up great; it took the plastic, it took shakers, it took, you name it, umbrellas, everything. I said, 'OK, take the horse away.'

About half an hour later the mother came back to me: 'It's doing it again.' 'Doing what?' 'Rearing and bucking – it won't go anywhere.' So I walked outside, and there's this horse going up, and buck, and up. It's got a gag in its mouth, and a drop noseband tying it down, and a set of spurs sending it forward. So she was pulling it, and it was going up; and kicking it, and it was bucking: it was doing exactly what she asked him. He was so clever.

I said, 'Look: take the noseband off it; take the spurs off it' – and, do you know? It never had a problem again. But officially, you have to ride in spurs. It's supposed to make the horse more alert, but what you are doing is prodding and prodding it in the guts with a lump of stainless steel – and that's with an animal so sensitive it can flick a fly off its body. What you are in danger of doing is bruising it and pissing it off. So you are taking the sensitivity you need out of an animal – and then wondering why you get so many problems . . .

But if you do get a horse that is rearing you need to be careful, because coming over backwards leads to the worst of injuries. I always say that the only times you should hit a horse is a smack round the hocks if it is kicking at you, or one round the fetlocks if it's rearing. When the horse rears, I actually slap the front legs below the knee and above the joint, so it's an instant pain. It won't want to feel that again – and anyway, to my eyes rearing is not a natural movement for the animal, except when it is a stallion covering. For if it goes up it is exposing its belly, and in the wild it would never do that, because all the lion or bear has to do is to rip its belly open and wait around for it to die.

Smacking the horse on the shins is like a swipe with a bear's claw, and it won't want to go up again and expose its belly. With fillies especially you want to stop rearing, because they are weaker behind, and more prone to falling over backwards if they go up with a rider on them. If they rear in the stalls, I get the jockey off and smack the horse on the shins if does it again. I had a case the other day: I smacked it on the shin, and next time it walked in first time. In two or three minutes it had got its confidence, and we had the jockey back on. The worst thing you want is the jockey having to be a hero before a horse is ready, because a horse who has lost his confidence in the stalls is a very dangerous thing.

A good example is Rex Imperator, who won the Stewards' Cup in 2013: he was the worst-behaved horse I have ever seen. He had always been a bit difficult when he was trained by Roger Charlton at Beckhampton. He would follow you three-quarters of the way into the stalls, back out a bit, and then plunge forward at you. At Doncaster, on his last run for Roger, he smashed my head up against the front, and George Baker, who rode him, hurt his leg, too. Then the horse was sold to run in Dubai and got very upset out there, and when he came back William Haggas sent him straight to me. He had gone: lost his confidence. He looked sad and hurt – just hated everybody, hated life.

Rex Imperator just didn't seem to care what he did – he would hurt anybody – and we had to put him on the floor to teach him manners. Eventually we got him going, but I wanted him to have a stalls test before he ran; it was Dubai where he had been chucked out, which meant officially he didn't need one here, nor was he entitled to one here, which is stupid, because a problem is a problem. Anyway, I go off to Kempton, and after a bit of hassle and me dropping the handlers £100 out of my own pocket, they let me take him down to the stalls after racing.

Well, he was a bastard. He completely lost the plot – he kicked the rails, he slammed into the front gate of the stalls. We put him in three or four times, but I thought there was no way we could run him like this. Simon McNeil, the starter, came up and said, 'F***ing hell, Gary – you've got no chance with this one. No chance – he just wants to kill everybody.' I thought, 'What do I do now?' so I ran to the car and got my chain halter and put it on him. And, do you know, he walked straight into the stalls and stood there. He absolutely stood there. Amazing.

My chain halter is not like the lip chain you used to see a lot of horses being led round the paddock with, that goes under the horse's lip and pulls up tight. That's like grabbing a tight hold of your nail: it's supposed to release endorphins and pacify the horse, but, as far as I am concerned, it is releasing pain – when horses are walking round with it, you can see their eyes almost crying with the pain. You used to see it used a lot; thankfully, not so much today. People might think my chain halter is severe, but it's not: it's actually quite light, and less severe than the rope halter, for the horses are only putting the pressure onto themselves. If they're walking quietly there is nothing on them at all, but if they start shooting off, the chain will tighten a bit, like a choker on a dog.

I have developed it in the last three or four years from something I saw in Dubai.

They cost about £60 to make up, and we always use a longer lead rope, because if a horse does rear up, a lot of the lead ropes are so short the animal gets away from you. I always use a three-metre length of rope, so if the horse does go up, the lead rope has got the length of the horse at full height, and when it comes back down, you've still got hold of it. The worst thing is letting the horse rear up and get away from you: then it has learned it can escape, and will certainly try it next time.

Sunday, August 4, 2013 **racingpost.com** **Racing Post** Sunday, August 4, 2013

Rex Imperator runs out a comfortable Stewards' Cup winner

Rex is Cup king for Haggas

▸▸Result Robins Farm Racing Stewards' Cup 6f

1 Rex Imperator ... 12-1
2 Ajjaadd ... 66-1
3 Burwaaz ... 25-1
4 Racy ... 16-1
5 Ninjago ... 8-1

Owner George Turner
Trainer William Haggas
Jockey Neil Callan
Groom Donovan Eldin
Breeder Christopher Mason
Distances 2¼l, ½l, ½l, hd

Graham Dench reports

REX IMPERATOR made a mockery of what looked a wide-open affair and gave William Haggas a second Stewards' Cup with a storming two-and-a-quarter-length defeat of outsider Ajjaadd.

It was only the four-year-old's fourth start for the stable, after jockey Neil Callan and a friend bought him from Roger Charlton last year on behalf of Callan's sponsor Steve Parkin and his associates with the Dubai International Carnival in mind. His trip there was a disaster, and he could finish only sixth when a strong fancy for Royal Ascot's Wokingham Handicap.

However, while George Turner, in whose colours Rex Imperator raced, unfortunately missed yesterday's Robins Farm Racing-backed cavalry charge after his plane had to make a forced landing at White Waltham, everything else slotted into place perfectly this time and the gelding travelled so strongly he could be named the winner long before he hit the front entering the final furlong.

A delighted Maureen Haggas, representing her husband, said: "You never think you are going to win one of these handicaps like that. They are hard to enough to win by a head [as the stable's Conquest did in 2008], let alone by two and a quarter, but Neil gave him a beautiful ride. He has to relax and travel and he did that today."

She added: "He went to Gary Witheford when he came back from Dubai and he and Donovan [Eldin], who rides him at home, have done a fantastic job. He had some good form when Roger [Charlton] had him, but I think he lost his confidence."

Asked if Rex Imperator's sights might be raised now, she replied: "After Conquest beat King's Apostle here they both went on to be Group horses, and he looked a nice prospect there."

Callan was with his family in Parkin's beach house at nearby Angmering when the Stewards' Cup draw was held on Thursday, but he told the trainer to go high and so was more than happy with stall 26.

Explaining the background behind the purchase, he said: "At the backend of last summer my sponsor asked me to find him a horse for the carnival and a friend and I sourced Rex Imperator.

"It didn't work out when he went to Dubai [raced once for David Nicholls] but we sent him to William when he came back and he needed those three runs for us to get to know him.

"He's highly strung but there's no badness in him, and after he was second at Windsor last time I knew the bigger field and stronger pace would suit him. Winning a race like that means a lot to me."

Rex Imperator denied the one-horse trainer Ted Powell a huge payday with Godolphin cast-off Ajjaadd, and it would not have been the Reigate stable's first success in one of the season's big handicaps. While his was not the name on the training licence when Hello Mister won back-to-back Portland Handicaps in 1994 and 1995, Powell bred the sprinter, who was trained under the name of Jack O'Donoghue before he got his own licence later in 1995.

Circumstances conspired against the seven-year-old here too, for Powell explained: "He is just too fast for them. He really likes a tow into his race but was up there. Even before this, the plan was the Portland. He wouldn't go for the Ayr Gold Cup though – that's too far to go!"

Jockey Willy Twiston-Davies confirmed: "He is a lot better when he gets a lead but we had to make it and couldn't get a tow. When the winner went by he started to find again."

Neil Callan (right) with Rex Imperator, whom he bought last year on behalf of his sponsor

On the way back from Kempton I rang William Haggas and said I was not happy with Rex Imperator, and that I would have to take him home and teach him some manners by working him with this chain on. William is a very organised man and told me to do whatever I wanted. Back home we got Rex into our round pen that same evening, laid him straight on the floor, and just walked away and left him. I let him lie there for a while – about five or six minutes: he thrashed around, but he couldn't get up because his legs were all tied. Then I went back to him, took the strap off, and walked him into the stalls. Well, the rest is history: he's been brilliant ever since, although he still doesn't enjoy being in the stalls very much, and we like to go last with him as we did when he won the Stewards' Cup. People say it's claustrophobia, but that's nonsense – no racehorse would go into those poky little partitions in a horse box if they had claustrophobia. What horses have when they go in the stalls is adrenalin bursting through their body, because they know they are about to run. And in Rex Imperator's case, run very fast.

That was a great day. William Haggas sent me a text saying, 'You're a genius', and his wife Maureen gave me a hug in the paddock and told the press it could not have happened without me. It's wonderful to be appreciated, and as a real rider she understands, but you would be amazed how ungrateful some trainers are. Of course, it's the job I get paid for, but 'thank you' does not cost any extra. It gets my goat when they don't say anything, especially if the success has been down to Craig.

That is just me being sensitive about the family because I suppose that part of my life will never get much better. After my mother died last year, my brother Chrissie found a letter from Reg Blakeley, apologising for what he and Tom had done. And not just apologising, but including details. It was a long letter: my mother had kept it all this time. It just broke us up, particularly Rob, because he hadn't fully realised about Reg before – he could not understand why Kevin had had him as best man at his wedding although Reg had never touched Kevin. Things got very unpleasant: I really thought Rob was going to do something terrible. Chrissie was so upset that he destroyed the letter. You could understand why at the time, but it would probably be enough evidence to send Reg and Tom back to jail today.

Yes, it never goes away, and the Rolf Harris case brought everything back and made it much worse again. For those men, those twins Reg and Tom Blakeley, took my childhood away. In many ways they took some of my life away, because the loving side, even in the sexual act, has really been taken away from me. It's not just me: all my brothers are affected, every one of us differently. It just shows that abuse inflicted on children stays with them as adults. It's no different from a baby yearling being abused: the memory stays with them. Horses will forgive, but they will never forget. I can't forgive what those twins did, and I'll never forget what they did.

What's worse is that they are both still around – they are in their seventies now – and they've both been in jail. Reg was locked up in Cambodia only a few years ago. Tom was in first – that was when my mother read out the piece in the paper – but he has got married since, and had a child. As recently as 2013 Reg was nailed by Mark Williams-Thomas, the man behind the exposure of Jimmy Savile, in an ITV programme called *Predators Abroad*, in which he tracks Reg down and confronts him in Torquay: there's a clip of it on YouTube, but I couldn't watch it – I'd be ill. Then only this August Chrissie went to an address where Tom was known to have lived in

2002-03. There was a woman in the garden, and when Chrissie began to say he was looking for some people who used to live around there, a man stepped from behind a tree. It was Tom. Chrissie saw right into his eyes. Tom knew it was him and stepped away. Chrissie told the woman he would ask further down the road. He's a big man Chrissie, but when he got to his car he was shaking. Those men need gelding, like we do with horses: they are still destroying people's lives. They're supposed to be Christian people, but they deserve to rot in hell for what they did.

As for me, I absolutely love my job. Most days I go away smiling with what I've achieved with horses. I'm not saying I've achieved much with people, but if there is a God, I thank him for what he has given me with horses, I really do. But with what happened to me as a child, and what's happened in my life, with the likes of my dad, and Cozy being killed, and Pauline's accident and all the rest, I think I've had to pay for what I have learned. Nothing comes easy in life: nothing is given to you without a price. You have to earn it.

I would like not have to work as physically hard as I do now for much longer. In 2007 I had a health scare: I was getting breathless, and a scan found a lump in my lung, a sarcoid, about the size of a grapefruit: they got it out, and said the condition was sarcoidosis and it could go either way. But Suze and I went to Brazil, and with the sunshine and the exercise the condition completely cleared up. But my body is beginning to fall to bits: I've had a lot of bangs in the stalls: I had my shoulder operated on at the start of the year, and I have cortisone injections every three months to keep me going. I am 54 now, and have thought for a while that if I hit 55 I will

be lucky. I would like it if I could go on for a few more years and bow out at the top. I don't want to get to the time where I have slowed down and get smashed up, and people see me walking round Lambourn looking for work.

I would like to go out on the road and teach. I would like to do a manual about starting stalls, to teach trainers and their staff so they could give their own horses a better deal. Just as every yard has a first-aider, so they could have someone trained by me. And why aren't the British Racing School or the BHA using me more? I've given talks at the School, but an apprentice there doesn't get taught properly about going through the stalls. There are all sorts of things we could do to improve the way horses are loaded: why don't these committees talk to someone who's working seven days a week solving problems in the stalls? I would love to to turn the TV on one day and see my tappers being used behind the stalls, and in the wider world

I would love to see horses having sensible bits in their mouths and people understanding them better.

I want to leave my mark. I think I have achieved something, but it is always a struggle with the old school, and it should never be 'this way or nothing': we all have something to give – if you've been around horses for 50 to 60 years you are going to have something to say to me about horsemanship. I've picked up lots of things along the way, but if we all put our little ideas into a pot we could learn together.

Though I have a big message out there, my horses have to do the talking. They are the innocent ones: it's what has always attracted me to them – they never lie like humans do, which is why we need to learn *their* language. It's not my language, it's *their* language: they want you to lead them, not muddle them up by treating them as humans.

For they are not humans: they are horses. And better for it.

TACK ROOM

Gary Witheford has the most challenging of stories and compelling of methods, and by far the best way of understanding what he does is to watch him in person or, failing that, watch the video footage on his website. Although in my direct experience his system is well-proven and his attitude appealing, still there needs to be a 'Do not try this at home' caveat about much of what you might see there; even more so in all you have just read.

For while the methods, the language, really do work, Gary is a unique product of years of very personal experience, and it is therefore more his overall attitude than any individual practices that I urge you to take from this book. To this end I am aware that not everyone will be familiar with all the phrases and terms that slip from his tongue, and indeed from many of us who are used to being around horses.

To help with that, I have attempted my own, sometimes somewhat discursive, explanations of all the key terms. I have tried to be neither patronising nor simplistic, on the long-held belief that you should neither over-estimate a reader's knowledge nor under-estimate their intelligence. And if some of you horsier folk scoff at me for explaining what spurs are, I bet you didn't know that Xenophon wrote about them in 400 BC.

ACP Acetyl prozamine – the most common form of horse tranquiliser. Commonly used to calm horses in stressful situations, but GW argues it merely masks problems which then emerge in 'undoped' situations the horse cannot handle.

Aga Khan Prince Karim Aga Khan, owner of one of the most successfully-run private stud operations in Britain and Ireland.

All-weather An artificial racing surface. In the UK it was pioneered in the 1980s to ensure jump racing in 'all weathers', but after a spate of accidents it was confined to the flat, with tracks at Lingfield, Kempton, Wolverhampton, Southwell and Newcastle (as from 2015).

Anchored A phrase used in racing when a jockey holds a horse firmly in at the rear of the field. Also used by GW in Chapter 13 in the same sense as 'parked' – to stand apparently loose but 'anchored to the the spot' by the weight of the knot at the end of the lead rope.

Andalusian Breed of Spanish horse recognised from the 15th century, and classically honoured as the horse ridden by Spanish knights. Andalusians are powerful and athletic, with thick manes and tails, and are often grey, as is GW's much-loved Andalusian, Brujo.

Apprentice An apprentice jockey – a teenager 'apprenticed' or indentured to a racing stable, on the supposition that in return for his labour he would be taught the rudiments of his profession and given opportunities to ride in races. In the past, too many trainers gained what was almost slave labour, by exploiting young men's dreams when there was never any serious intention of their becoming jockeys. That practice no longer continues.

Backing The process of getting a horse accustomed to having a rider on his back. It used to take weeks: with GW's method of winning a horse's confidence it can take only a few minutes.

Bay A mid to light brown horse with a black mane and tail. A very dark brown horse is called a 'brown'. Black horses exist but are comparatively rare.

Bit The piece of metal, usually of steel, held in the horse's mouth by the bridle. The rings of the bit are attached to the reins with which the rider steers and controls the horse.

Blindfold Put over a horse's head to help load it into the starting stalls. The idea is that, once disorientated and pacified, it will co-operate more readily. See also 'hood'.

Blinkers Horse's headgear slipped over the ears and containing cupped plastic eyepieces which allow forward but prevent backward vision. In racing these are seen as an aid to concentration and a 'hurry-up'. But in carriage days they were seen as a pacifier, to stop the horse worrying about the vehicle behind. Gary uses them in the latter role, for nervous horses in the 'starting' process.

Bolt	To run away uncontrollably. Used with horses it usually involves having a rider on board. With humans normally applied to errant wives or husbands.
Box walker	A nervous horse who has got into the habit of pacing up and down in his box, thus impairing his condition.
Breaking-in	The process of teaching a horse to accept first a bridle and saddle, and then the instructions of the rider on his back. GW likes to call it 'starting'.
British Horseracing Authority (BHA)	The regulatory body for British racing since 2007, and, as such, responsible for rules governing starting-stalls procedures amongst many other things.
British Racing School	Established at Newmarket in 1983: runs courses for stable staff, jockeys and trainers. GW went to a less-organized forerunner at the National Equestrian Centre at Stoneleigh in Warwickshire. See Chapter 3 and smile.

Buck Brannaman Dan M. 'Buck' Brannaman, born in Wisconsin in 1962, is one of the great figures of the Natural Horsemanship movement. A disciple of Ray Trott, who in turn had learned from Tom Dorrance in Oregon and Montana, Brannaman was the principal inspiration for Nicholas Evans' bestselling *The Horse Whisperer*, and was Robert Redford's double in the film.

Call-up GW's phrase for the horse/man link-up at the end of 'the Points' routine. See 'Join-Up'.

Canter In normal riding this is the rocking gait only marginally faster than the trot. In the racehorse it's fast enough to be a gallop in layman's terms, but is still only 60% of full speed for a thoroughbred.

Cavesson Normally the name for a standard noseband – from the italian *cavazzone* or halter – but here meaning the harder, ringed noseband used in the traditional 'breaking-in' process.

Chain halter A form of halter devised by GW, which tightens with pressure, but releases when the horse walks forward.

Changing legs The action of a horse switching its leading leg at the canter. If it is going round any sort of corner it needs to lead with the inside leg: hence it will need to 'change legs' if GW reverses its direction in the round pen.

Chifney A bit used to lead stallions and potentially fractious horses. It slips over the mouth and has such a severe operation that it is never used for actual riding. It was invented by the legendary jockey Samuel Chifney, whose talent was only matched by his conceit – witness the title of his 1795 autobiography, *Genius Genuine*.

Claiming hurdle A race over hurdles. A 'claiming' race is one in which the owner is prepared to part with his horse for a stipulated amount – 'the claiming price'. Good horses are therefore unlikely to run for fear of them being 'claimed' for far below their real value; hence, these races offer winning chances to the lesser lights. The same system is often used on the Flat, and the races often referred to as 'claimers'.

Clipping/clippers Electric clippers, resembling a giant electric razor. They are used to shave back the longer coat that horses grow in the winter months, and so avoid them sweating excessively during exercise.

Coloured Refers to a horse's coat: a collective term covering 'piebald' (black and white), or 'skewbald' (brown and white). In the UK most commonly associated with a skewbald, which in the USA is referred to as Pinto.

Colt A male horse who has not taken up reproduction – when it is termed a stallion – or been castrated, in which eunuch state it is termed a 'gelding'.

Connemara A strong and athletic, medium-sized Irish pony evolved as a breed in the Connemara district around County Galway in western Ireland. Connemaras are often grey, measure between 13 and 15 hands, and are said to owe some part of their origins to Andalusian horses shipwrecked from the defeated Spanish Armada in 1588.

Crupper	A strap attached to the back of a saddle which ends with a loop under the horse's tail to prevent the saddle from slipping forwards. These are necessary with donkeys, mules and some ponies who do not have round enough shoulders. But they were also often used on yearlings in the 'breaking' process. See Chapter 6.
Cut	A euphemism for 'castrate', or even 'geld', as in 'castrating' or 'gelding' a colt, which is then referred to as a 'gelding'.
Dam	A horse's female parent.
De-flight	GW's phrase for his way of calming very nervous horses. They are animals of flight, so by showing them they won't receive any harm from 'clippers' or 'plastic' or other fears, he wins their confidence and takes the 'flight' out of them.
Dipped back	An aberration of horse conformation, but not always totally detrimental to its athletic prowess.
Doing a horse	A racing term for a stable lad for taking responsibility for an individual horse – as in, Gary 'did' Alpenstock, Royal Mail and Son Of A Gunner.
Done over	Groomed. In a good racing stable each horse is groomed or 'done over' every evening. Its feet would be picked out, its mane and tail brushed, and in particular its coat groomed gleamingly clean, so that the white glove of a trainer like Jeremy Tree (chapter 2) could not pick up a speck of dirt.
Door-slamming	A metaphor used by GW for the part of his 'Points' routine when he challenges the circling horse to make it turn and go in the opposite direction: he is 'slamming the door'.

Double Diamond halter	The make of rope halter used by GW and marketed by Buck Bannaman. With its half-hitch knots, pressure is applied if the horse pulls back, but released the moment he moves forward.

Dressage	An equestrian discipline somewhere between ballet and gymnastics on horseback.
Elephant trunk	GW's description of a horse's facial demeanour in Chapter 16 : 'When they are angry that top lip goes all stiff – I call it the "elephant trunk".'
Equiground	The artificial surface on which GW's first 'round pen' was established at Wootton Bassett.
Equus	Monty Roberts' version of the horse language referred to in 'Natural Horsemanship', and also the name of the horse show in London's Docklands where GW performed in 2002.

False start The start of a horse race which has been judged faulty because certain runners have charged the starter's call to go. The runners will be called back to try again.

Felt padded sticks The standard UK racing whip, now usually made with a fibreglass inner stem wrapped in folded patent vinyl. It makes a noise on impact, but is too padded to cause any harm.

Fetlock The joint connecting the cannon bone and the pastern – sometimes referred to as the 'ankle'. The human analogy is not actually correct: to be exact, the fetlock is a metacarpophalangeal joint which corresponds to the human upper knuckle, such as that on the ball of the foot. Bet you didn't know that . . .

Filly In most equestrian disciplines a female horse is termed a filly until it is four years old, when it is called a mare; in racing it stays a 'filly' until it is five. If it conceives, it then becomes a 'brood mare'.

First lot The first group of horses to go out from a racing stable in the morning. This will often be very close to daybreak, especially in winter.

Flash noseband A second strap is attached to the bottom of the normal plain noseband, and taken down and round the horse's chin below the bit. Since it keeps the bit firmly in the horse's mouth, it is seen as giving more leverage to a rider than a plain snaffle, thus making it easier to control a horse who is 'pulling' hard.

Flight The default 'escape' attitude of a horse when scared. Handling this is central to GW's theories. See 'deflight'.

Flight or fight The two options a horse usually adopts when 'pressured' in the round pen. If it is 'fight', the man must not back down.

Floor Tied See also 'park'. GW's system whereby a knot is tied in a horse's lead rope and with that little extra weight a horse will rest it on the ground and stay 'parked' or 'floor tied'. In GW's yard horses are not normally tied to rings in the standard way.

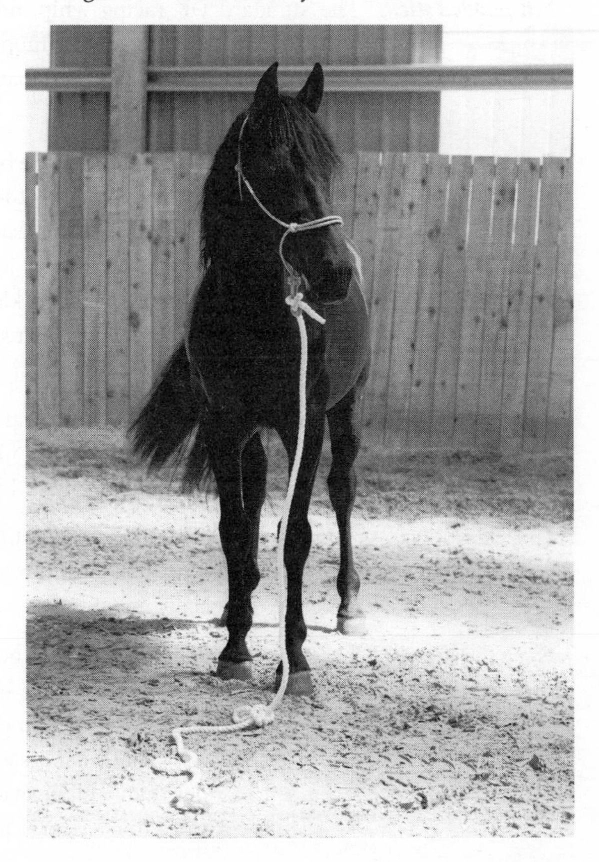

Forsmanship The name for the version of 'Natural Horsemanship' developed by Stefan Forsman in Sweden, and the system most influential on GW.

Furlong Imperial unit of measurement used in the British Empire and traditionally in horse racing, there being eight furlongs to the mile. A furlong, therefore, being 220 yards. However, most countries except England and Ireland, have gone metric – Australia back in 1972. Since a furlong is actually 201.168 metres this means that the rounded-up metric equivalents to horse-racing distances are always slightly less – as in five furlongs compared to 1,000 metres, when the equivalent distance is actually 1,005.84 metres.

Gary Witheford rug See 'Stalls rug'.

Godolphin The name given by Sheikh Mohammed to his racing stable in Dubai, which has become one of the world's most successful international racing operations. The name derives from the Godolphin Arabian, one of the trio of foundation sires of the thoroughbred from which all racehorses derive. Originally from the Yemen, he came into the ownership of Lord Godolphin, and was kept at his lordship's stud near the splendidly-named Gog Magog Hills, near Cambridge.

Group One race The highest category of flat race – as in Classics like the Derby. See 'Listed race'.

Hack Employed as a noun, the word 'hack' means a horse used merely for leisure, non-competitive and usually non-jumping exercise. The verb denotes doing the same thing on horseback. As an adjective, in 'hack canter', it means the slowest, gentlest form of canter.

Half-bred General term for a horse one of whose parents is a thoroughbred – hence 'half-bred'.

Hands As in 'It was a white pony, not very big, about 12 hands.' The 'hand' is a unit of measurement standardised at four inches in 1541 by a statute of King Henry VIII. The rest of the world uses the metric system, with the exception of the UK, USA, Ireland, Canada and Australia, even though the last-named otherwise went metric in 1972.

Hanoverian A powerful type of middle-weight horse originally bred in the Hanover region Germany (the clue is in the name). Once prized as the best type of coach horse, Hanoverians are now much in demand for dressage, show jumping and eventing, in each of which three disciplines they have won Olympic gold. They are termed 'warm bloods', as opposed to 'cold bloods' (heavy cart horses), or 'hot bloods' (Arabs or thoroughbreds).

Have this off Slang term for landing a gamble – traditionally involving knowing more about your horse's ability than others, and most especially the bookmakers.

Hobbles Linked ankle cuffs used as a means of restraint and in some territories as a prevention against straying.

Hocks Elbow joints in the hind leg of a horse. 'Getting back on his hocks' is a phrase for gathering a horse together – especially before a jump.

Home bred Bred and reared by the owner, as opposed to bought at the sales as a foal, yearling or two-year-old.

Hood When covering ears and eyes it is used to disorientate a horse that refuses to go into the starting stalls. Also used with just the ears covered to keep extra sound away from nervous horses.

Hot-branded Scarring a permanent mark or lettering onto a horse to signify ownership by pressing a red-hot iron into its coat. It is a painful procedure which, as in Brujo's case, can leave a scar on the brain as well as the skin.

Irons As in 'stirrup irons'. Nowadays of steel or aluminium, these are the door-shaped frames attached to the saddle by the 'stirrup leather' on which a rider's feet balance while in the saddle. 'Standing up in the irons' means lifting your backside from the saddle and so balancing only on the 'irons'.

Join-Up The phrase used by Monty Roberts for the moment in 'Natural Horsemanship' when the horse chooses to be with the human, and walks toward him/her, accepting their leadership and protection. In GW's version it is referred to as 'Call-Up, but the essence is the same.

Kicking distance The range at which a horse could hit you if it lashed out with its hind legs. Usually seen as six to eight feet. Hence the use of 'tappers' from the side to encourage a horse to move forward into the stalls rather than standing behind in kicking range.

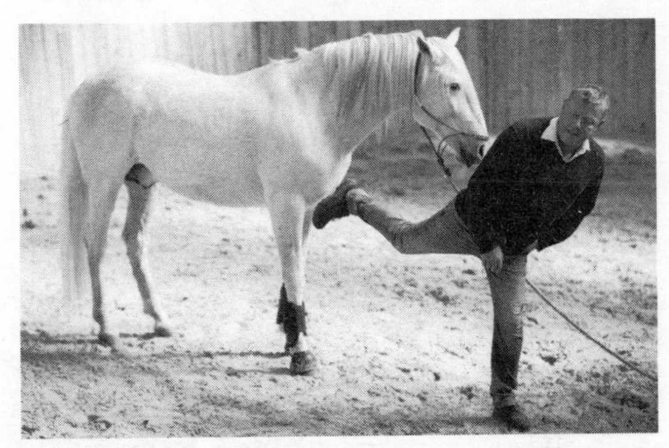

Kissing sound The 'Go on' sound GW uses to command horses in the round pen and outside. Also used with reluctant stalls-horses and horses that nap. The kiss is another form of pressure and means move.

Kissing spine A horse with this condition feels consistent, low-grade pain because the spinous processes, or sections of bone attached to the vertebrae, are too close together and impinge on one another.

Lead rope The rope with which a horse is led – usually from a head collar. GW's lead ropes are 3 metres long. He believes short ropes make it easier for a horse to break free if it bucks or rears, and once it has done so will try and repeat it .

Leg strap Leather strap – usually a stirrup leather, used to buckle a horse's raised foreleg back into the same limb and so bring a fractious horse under control.

Leopardstown Irish racetrack on the southern outskirts of Dublin, with the Wicklow mountains as a handsome backdrop.

Lick and chew The movement of the lips, which, along with the dipping of the head, indicates passivity in the horse, and in an instructional context is the cue that he is ready for the next command.

Lippizaner The classical breed, often grey, founded by the Hapsburg nobility in 16th-century Slovenia, and most famous as the horse of choice for the Spanish Riding School in Vienna.

Listed race A category of flat race one below Group Three. Group Two is one above Group Three, and Group One the highest class.

Load To put a horse into something, as in 'loading' into a horse box or the starting stalls.

Long rein As the name suggests, these are long (up to 10 metre) reins, attached to the bridle, held not by the rider in the saddle but by a 'driver' walking behind, as in the image of the ploughman.

Long Tom A whip with a long lash. Originally used by starters to encourage horses reluctant to line up before a race, but not permitted now for fear of TV viewers taking offence. GW still believes in the flick, when necessary, around the hocks to stop a kicker, and on the forelegs to prevent rearing.

Lunge To 'lunge' a horse is to exercise it in a circle at the end of a long rein – the latter is then referred to as a 'lunge rein'.

Lunge line A long – 20-metre – canvas line attached to a horse's head collar, so enabling the 'lunger' to make the horse circle around him.

Lusitano The Portugese breed of horse so similar to the Andalusian that until 1966 they were considered the same breed. Once established as a separate breed such horses were given the name Lusitano after the Roman name for Portugal, Lusitania.

Martingale A piece of tack designed to check a horse's head carriage. A 'standing martingale' runs direct from the girth to the bottom of the noseband, and the 'running martingale' goes from the girth to rings attachd to the reins. Obviously the 'standing martingale' is the more direct corrective.

Meydan Dubai's astonishing premier racetrack. Opened in March 2010 it has become the home of the world's richest race, the $10m Dubai World Cup, and has a grandstand that is 1 mile, yes, 1 mile long.

Monty Roberts' rug A rug with padded sides to help horses wary of banging their own sides against the steel structure of the stalls. Monty Roberts first used his 'rug' in the UK in 1992. See 'Stalls rug'.

Mouth The responsiveness of a horse to the bit. An unresponsive animal is termed as having a 'hard' mouth, and a sensitive one a 'light' mouth.

Myler Bit GW's preferred bit as opposed to the Snaffle. Unlike the Snaffle it has a central link and so avoids the 'nutcracker' action on the roof of the horse's mouth when the rider pulls on the 'Snaffle'.

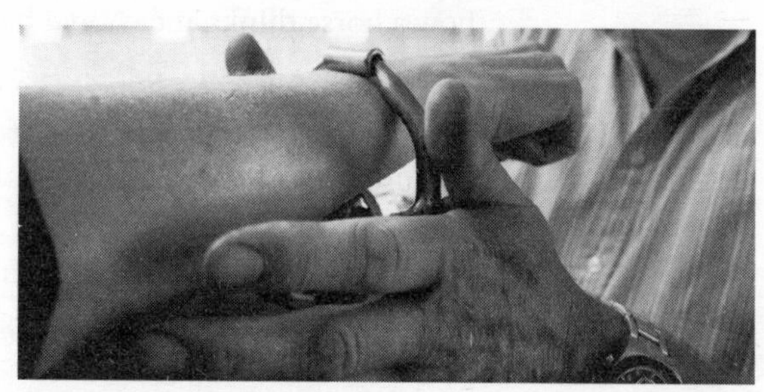

Myler bit

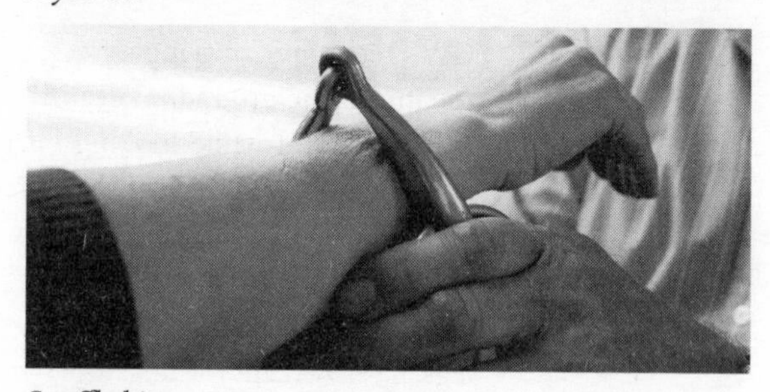

Snaffle bit

Nappy As in 'The pony Snoopy who had gone all nappy.' Equine slang for a horse who has become disobedient and 'naps', or throws some sort of tantrum, instead of doing what it is asked.

Natural Horsemanship The generic term used by Gary for his methods, and deriving from the western United States, where the concept was first developed in the latter half of the last century by Tom Dorrance in Oregon. His disciple Ray Hunt was followed by Buck Bannaman, who was the principal inspiration for Nicholas Evans' bestselling book *The Horse Whisperer*, and also Robert Redford's double in the film. Following the book and film 'Natural Horsemanship' became synonymous with 'Horse Whispering', and while individual exponents such as the famous Monty Roberts and Pat Parelli may differ on details, the central idea advocates a better understanding of how a horse thinks and should be educated.

Near fore The front left leg of a horse. The right-hand side is referred to as the 'off side'; the left is the 'near side', because all activities like leading, bridling, saddling and mounting are done from the near side. Except, that is, in the film *War Horse* when, irredeemably, horses were often depicted being led on from the right-hand side – presumably for better, albeit totally inauthentic, film shots.

On the floor GW's technique of tying a horse's legs so that it has to sink to the ground. He calls it 'putting them on the floor', and while looking fairly brutal, actually involves no violence, as if the horse does struggle it is only struggling against its trussed-up self. GW's theory, and achievement, is that the horse, once realising you have taken away his greatest asset, his legs, has to accept the absolute truth that it is not he but the man who should be the leader.

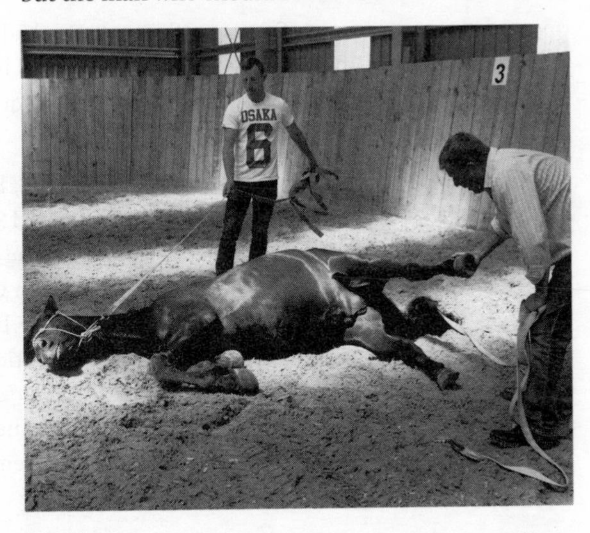

Pad A piece of protective padding to be placed under the saddle to prevent pain and chafing.

Park Used as a transitive verb, as in 'to park' a horse – part of GW's technique when leading a horse. Once the horse has accepted the role of walking a metre and a half behind the man he is checked to a standstill, a knot is tied in the lead rope, so that if the horse drops its head, the knot will rest on the ground. It will stay there, 'parked', for the duration. There are no tie-rings to attach ropes to at GW's stables. See also 'Floor Tied'.

Percheron A French version of our Shire horse. GW helped with two Percherons called Manet and Rodin, owned by *Sunday Times* writer Jonathan Miller.

Pessoa The Pessoa is a training aid aimed at making a horse flex its neck and back in a controlled manner on the lunge (see picture). It is a series of attachments to the bridle and girth on either side of the horse which are taken back to support a strap under the quarters. GW uses it for both control and recuperation.

Picador The mounted figure in a bullfight who does not try and evade the bull, but draws him on to attack his blindfolded and padded horse, giving the picador the chance to drive his lance into the bull's neck muscles and so lower its head to allow the matador's sword a place to penetrate. The horse's predicament is among the most upsetting images in the equestrian world.

Piebald A black-and-white horse. See 'coloured'.

Pirouette While the word is often used for any sort of spinning turn by a horse, done properly it is one of the finest movements in dressage – the horse turning on its hind quarters, while its forelegs spin round faster to keep the hind legs on the spot.

Plastic Large pieces of plastic sheeting – used by GW to rub and crinkle to desensitise horses' natural fear of the material, and to cover them with, as part of his 'de-flighting' treatment.

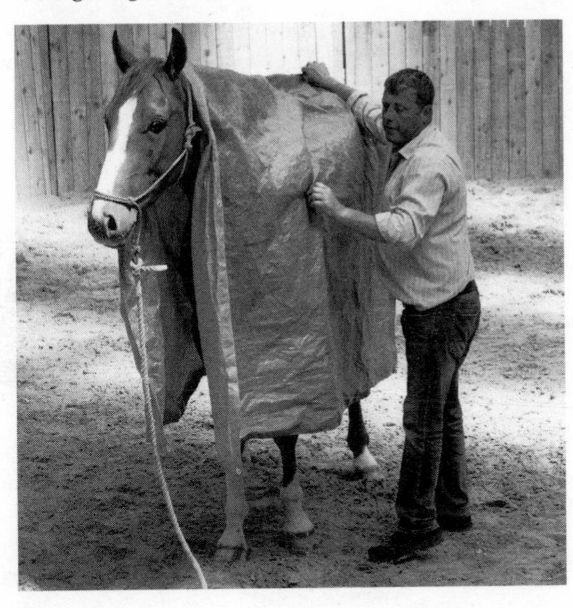

Pool money	In a racing stable, such as Stan Mellor's where GW was, a percentage of the stable's winnings would be put into a 'pool', which would be shared out as a Christmas bonus. The current deduction is 3% .
Post and rails	The traditional wooden fencing used on stud farms. The posts are usually six feet apart, and there are three lines of rails, the highest circa 4 feet 6 inches, which should contain all but the most errant quadruped.
Pressure/release	The main 'dialogue' mechanism used by GW. At the most basic, if you are doing halter work, you ask the horse to walk towards you using the rope (pressure), when the horse moves forwards you stop using the rope (release). If you tap a horse from behind (pressure) and it walks forward, you stop tapping immediately (release). You reward it for accepting your command. The human has to be the leader and apply the pressure, but to be trusted the pressure must be released as soon as the horse agrees to the command.
Prix de L'Arc de Triomphe	France's, and Europe's, greatest flat race, run over a mile and a half at Longchamp in Paris on the first Sunday in October.
Pusher	Someone who helps push a horse into the stalls. GW never normally uses 'pushers', having taught his horses to follow where he leads.
Quarter horse	An American breed developed to race over just a quarter of a mile. It evolved from the horses used by cowboys, for whom sprint speed to 'cut out' errant cattle was the most coveted of assets.
Quarter marks	Patterns made on a horse's hindquarters at the end of grooming. Stable lads like to do it for a bit of a show, and possibly to win a 'best turned-out' award at the races.

Quick Release Head Collar Used to help horses into the starting stalls. Once loaded, time is of the essence, with one press on the side this head collar drops away.

Rear (reared/ rearing) The act of a horse standing up on its hind legs. It is an extremely dangerous habit in ridden horses, as it can end with them slipping over backwards on top of the rider.

Riding out Riding exercise for a racehorse trainer. The horses are usually described as a 'string', and individual groups as 'lots' – 'first lot' being earliest, etc.

Roller A fully-encircling girth. Sometimes used to keep stable rugs in place, or as part of the 'breaking-in' process to ready the horse for the feel of the saddle. Needless to say, GW has dispensed with it.

Round pen	The 60-foot-diameter enclosure in which GW does his teaching.
Sacking	As part of GW's 'de-flighting' process he would rub and bang horses with sacks, hence 'sacking'.
School (noun)	Manège, as in 'indoor school'.
School (verb)	Educate – usually in manège, sometimes 'over fences'.
Shakers	Large plastic bottles in which GW shakes old stones to cause a scary-sounding rattle. They are part of the 'de-flighting' process in which horses get so used to such things that they will even stand still while a whip is cracked near their head.

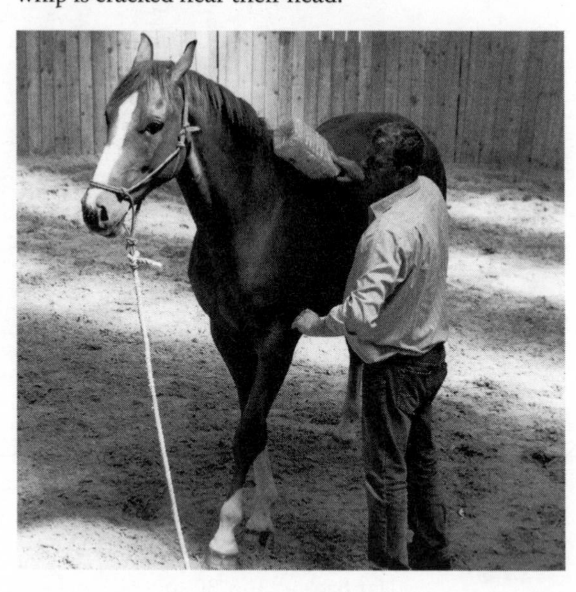

Sheepskin cheek pieces	Thick rolls of sheepskin placed on the bridle to block backward vision . See 'blinkers.'
Sire	Used as a noun it denotes a horse's male parent. As a verb it means the act of begetting. Derived from the Latin 'senior', and traditionally used to address monarchs and nobility.

Skewbald A brown and white horse. See 'coloured'.

Slasher attacks Series of night-time knife attacks in the summer of 2005 on three of GW's foals. No culprit was ever caught, but the police thought the motives were more perversion than criminal.

Snaffle The most common bit used with a horse's bridle. It is generally considered the mildest of bits but, as related in chapter 16, GW disagrees, saying the jointed mouthpiece applies a 'nutcracker' action.

Spurs Metal prods buckled to the heels of riding boots, with the aim of encouraging the horse forward. They are used in most horse disciplines and are compulsory in some. They are mentioned by Xenophon as far back as 400 BC, but GW believes the equestrian establishment is outdated in not opposing them. See Chapter 16.

Stallion Male horse whose main role in life is reproduction – physically they develop more crested necks, and behaviourally they are much more tactile with their teeth.

Stalls (starting stalls, stalls test/ Steriline) Partitioned steel pens from which all flat races are now started In the UK. They were first used on 1 July 1939 at Exhibition Park, Vancouver, British Columbia, to a design by a former jockey and starter called Clay Puett. The trial was an immediate success, and by the end of 1940 the starting gate was a fixture at all major North American race tracks, but typical British conservatism prevented its use in the UK until 1965.

Stalls rug The slip off rug which GW uses to help some horses enter the starting stalls. It has padding in the sides to stop a horse's ribs or hips from bumping the hard edges of the stalls. Gary's version is smaller and lighter but equally as padded as the Monty Roberts version. It is designed to be less hot to wear and less cumbersome to leave behind when the horse jumps from the stalls.

Standing bars in stalls Narrow ledges inside the starting stalls on which the jockeys rest their feet if the horse gets fractious, or they themselves just want to stand apart.

Starting	GW's preferred word for the 'breaking-in' process of educating of a horse to saddle and rider.
Steriline starting stalls	The new Australian design of starting stalls introduced to the UK in 2005, initially causing injury and controversy in which GW was heavily involved, as recounted in Chapter 13. See also 'Stalls'.
Stifle	The joint high up on the front of a horse's hind leg. It is taken as the line from below which the flank of the horse is 'trace clipped'.
Strapping	The grooming act of massaging right across the body of the horse. Traditionally this was done with a 'wisp': a rolled-up bunch of moistened straw that would be banged against a horse's neck or side and then 'strapped' across its body. Not many stables or stable employees have the time to do it now. Gary always did.
Tappers	Light and narrow three-foot-long modified lunge whips used to 'tap' the horse on either side of the hindquarters, to encourage it forward either into a horsebox or (at GW's stables) into the starting stalls. By standing either side, one can lessen the danger of being kicked, and help keep the hindquarters straight. GW disagrees with the BHA ban on racecourse 'tappers', a pandering to the sensibilities of TV viewers.

The Hennessy Hennessy Gold Cup – a major 3¼ mile steeplechase run at Newbury and now the oldest continuous sponsorship in the game.

The Points The driving-and-turning educational exercise in the round pen which is at the centre of GW's method to achieve 'Call-Up'. The horse is made to turn at each of the ring's four quarters, in a routine a bit like driving it through a maze, in which you open and shut doors to lead it out the other side. By the time the horse has finished, it will accept the human as 'leader'. See page 114.

Thoroughbred The thoroughbred racehorse: the worldwide breed established through the 17th and 18th centuries by crossing Engish mares with imported stallions from the Middle East. By the early 18th century the breed had evolved into the fastest weight-carrying creature the world has ever seen, and with its spread round the globe can be counted Britain's greatest gift to the animal kingdom. What are the other contenders?

Toothy A phrase given to male horses, especially colts, and most especially stallions. In the wild the stallion uses his teeth both for fighting and for holding on to the mane of the mare while mating. Many stallions are so 'toothy' that grooms carry big wooden sticks with them for stallions to put their teeth on.

Top weight In 'handicap races' an attempt is made to equalise the chance of each horse by allocating it more or less weight in ratio to its ability. So the best horse would carry 'top weight' – usually no more than 10 stone in flat racing, or 12 stone over jumps.

Twine	Standard twine, usually of sisal, used to bind up bales of hay. It is very strong but can be cut and disposed of easily – perfect for GW to adapt bridles, as with Winston. (Chapter 16)

Twitch	A loop, usually of cord, which is put round a horse's top lip and then twisted tight so as to incapacitate it. Although it is used in many stables Gary believes it is too severe – see Chapter 5.
Unbroken	Horse as yet unused to being saddled and ridden. See 'breaking in' and 'starting.'
White stocking	White hair on the legs of a horse. Historically there was a degree of prejudice against them – and a famous jingle: 'One white sock, buy him. Two white socks, try him. Three white socks, give him to your wife. Four white socks, run for your life.' The idea, unproven, is that white stockings show a weakness in the bone.
Wither	As in Royal Mail's 'very high wither'. The withers are the ridge between a horse's shoulder blade and the point at which a horse's height is measured. They are the highest consistent part of the horse, as they cannot be lowered like the head and neck.

Working a horse 'loose'	Driving a horse around a ring without any contact. This is the foundation of Gary's 'Points' system of establishing bonds between man and horse.
Yearling	Horses are usually foaled in the spring. They are termed 'foals' until the end of that calendar year, when they are termed yearlings, subsequently two-year-olds and so on. Whatever their foal date, they become a yearling on their first 1 January.

Acknowledgements

Gary Witheford has many great qualities but sitting down to pen long books has not as yet been amongst them. However, from when we first met I was struck by both his passion and by the untutored eloquence with which he told his tales. The more I got to know of his story the more I felt that it should be told, however painful some of the recollections might be.

Long hours with the tape recorder, including one epic journey to and from York races, produced a seed corn from which we have tried to produce a book which is authentic and challenging as well as a portrait of a remarkable life. But to know where to get a sense of perspective I needed guidance from those who have been with Gary along the way. So in what is hopefully a self explanatory order I would like to thank the generous input of: Chris Witheford, Alan Stonell, Stan and Elain Mellor, Eric Wheeler, Reg and Gill Dixon, Kevin Mooney, Philip Blacker, Simon Tindall, Dr Desmond Morris, Sylvia and John Froome, Sue Bond, Josie Lewis, Nicky Davies, Jacqui Broadbridge, Sarah and Will Long, Simon McNeill, Lady Carnarvon, James Doyle, Harry Dunlop, Brendan Powell, William Haggas, Archie Watson, John Gosden, Kelvin McKenzie, Benson Craven, Chris McDowell, and very especially for his humour and forbearance with my endless queries about his dad – Craig Witheford.

We have been hugely helped by the team put together by James de Wesselow at Racing Post Books. They included Sterling Transcription who wrote up the tapes, Anthony Dunkley and Vanessa Mallinson who supported me in the search for structure, Graham Coster who took on a first draft of the manuscript, John English who took over the final proofs, Jay Vincent for his memorable cover design and above all to John Schwartz whose ability to 'get' what an author is after and link it to pictures and design has never been more brilliant – especially as this was done in swimming shorts from his seaside cottage in New England.

Julian Brown has been a rock in the publishing office just as Gill Heaney has been in my own but the final delivery belongs to Liz Ampairee whose drive knows no limits when a book and a dodgy author are in the way and to Gary's wife Suzanne whose industry and patience is nothing short of astonishing. She not only made the book possible but she and Gary and all the team at Westcourt made the project one of the most enjoyable and uplifting experiences I have ever had.

Brough Scott
September 2014

I never dreamt my story would ever really be printed and am genuinely amazed we finally got here. I really want to thank all the amazing animals and of course the people that have helped me along the way – they know who they are and they are too numerous to name but I want to say thanks to a few in particular.

My family, especially my children, Gemma, Callie and Craig who, I know, have most certainly gone without my attention at times when I have been devoted to my life with horses.

Brough for managing to make sense of the endless conversations and stories from the past, my life today and my hopes for the future. I believe he has done it in a way that will help readers to understand what makes me tick.

James, Liz, Julian and all the team at Racing Post Books, of course!

Alan Stonell for saving me in my younger years and for pointing me in the right direction and Eric Wheeler for his continued support and for being the nearest thing to a father I have.

My staff, past and present – especially the ever faithful Nicky Davies. I know I can be difficult sometimes but those who truly know me understand why and those that don't, well perhaps they'll understand more when they have read this.

Suze for standing by me through thick and thin; she knows I appreciate her really, I just don't always show it!

Craig for being by my side and sometimes even ahead of me – what a man he has become and I am very, very proud of him.

To all the horses – especially Bold Start Lady who was there at the beginning, Arnie who I met along the way and finally to Brujo – I hope he stays around for a long time.

Gary Witheford
September 2014

Index

Page numbers in *italics* refer to illustrations.